WRINKLES WELCOME

WRINKLES WELCOME

A Cancer Survivor's Memoir

GABY LAURENT

ILLUMIFY
MEDIA.COM

Wrinkles Welcome

Copyright © 2024 by Gaby Laurent

This is a true story of my lived experience. Some names and details have been changed.

Published by

Illumify Media Global

www.IllumifyMedia.com

"Let's bring your book to life!"

Paperback ISBN: 978-1-964251-12-7

Cover photography by Shauna McCoy

Cover design by Debbie Lewis

Printed in the United States of America

For my mother, who crossed an ocean
to keep me safe.

CONTENTS

*I*NTRODUCTION

Would you poison your baby? What if they were still inside your body? Would you allow anything in that could negatively affect them? Most people would answer a resounding "NO!" With the existing research we have on mothers-to-be and babies, we know to stay away from soft cheese, alcohol and deli meat. It is easy to avoid raw sushi, meat, or eggs for nine months; that is no sacrifice. I don't even like tartare.

But I had to make the terrible decision to poison my baby. When I was twenty-six, I experienced the euphoria of discovering I was pregnant. However, this revelation was quickly undercut by the detection of cancer in routine blood work performed at my OB-GYN office. Not just any cancer, but the one Hollywood depicts as a death sentence: leukemia.

I was forced to make a terrible decision, one that no one should have to make. My options were bleak, but I chose to begin chemotherapy while my baby was in utero. This was the only way for both of us to survive, and that was not guaranteed.

I clung to my faith and family. I had to believe God would write a story of wonder through me. What I witnessed was a string of miracles, all compounding on each other, all pointing my heart back to one thing: hope. This hope carried me through bringing home two babies, each with their own incredible stories. Stories that I pray will help you realize that hope is worth fighting for; it is worth believing in.

In walking a path that should have ended in death, I learned that even on my worst or most boring day, life is a gift. Today is all we have; let's make the most of it. Turn on some music and dance in the kitchen. If this moment is all there is, we might as well learn to enjoy it, to have our hands splayed open to the possibilities of it. If more time on Earth is my greatest achievement, I must take all that comes with it. The highs and lows and the in-between. If I am lucky enough to collect such a copious amount of days that my face shifts, that it sags and furrows, with creases and spots, I must accept it all. The inevitable changes to my precious body require me to say, "Wrinkles welcome." For if I have a face full of wrinkles, that means only one thing: I am alive.

The book you are about to read is not the book I intended to write. I was going to tell you about my experience with cancer and how it changed my life. In writing my memoir, I made discoveries about myself that I'd missed along the way while living my life. For the last nine years, my hands have been full, taking care of babies and making sure I drink enough water.

INTRODUCTION

Only in sitting still, hours at a time, pondering my past
did the full picture make itself known.

Back in 2015, when I was finished with treatment
and began the crawl back to the land of the living,
people asked me the same question: "How did you
survive?" My response was always an effort to lift the
other person: "I did what I had to do. You would have
done the same. You are much stronger than you think."

Now, this is true—you, precious reader, are stronger
than you think—but there is more to my survival story
than sheer gumption.

I am the luckiest girl in the world; I won the lottery
the day I was born. I lived in the safest and most loving
home, in the middle of a retired tobacco farm in rural
North Carolina. With a multicultural family, my mother
from Costa Rica and my father from Stokes County,
North Carolina, I learned quickly that there is beauty
in diversity. We were raised to be frugal, to know how
to work with our hands. We were taught to respect our
elders, say por favor and thank you. But most impor-
tantly, I was given a rich inheritance through my family
tree. You may have images of Scrooge McDuck diving
into pools of gold and jewels, but what I was granted is
better than anything money can buy.

The specific combination of accouterments given
to me by my parents and grandparents was necessary
for me to survive. I needed a deep well to draw from
that would never go dry. With all my ancestors rooted
in their faith in God, I too, became fully prepared for
what was to come my way.

PART 1

CANCER

1

LOVE AND SAFETY

In 1983 a young man followed a still, small voice 3,555 miles; from the foothills of North Carolina, he traveled to the city of San Jose, Costa Rica. He intended to help put a roof on a small church. But God had other plans. While there he met a beautiful young lady, and they fell in love. After writing letters back and forth and spending every Friday night on long-distance phone calls, they decided to get married. After a whirlwind of paperwork and visits to the U.S. Embassy in Costa Rica, they were able to get married and begin their life together in North Carolina.

These two people brought their distinct backgrounds together, a city girl from Central America and a country boy from Stokes County, to create something unimaginable. The safest home, where every person who came through the doors felt seen and heard. This was my foundation for life. Two imperfect people who found each other and, with the help of God, discovered how to live in peace with each other and the world around them.

I always knew my existence hinged on their faith and the tiny chance that they, living countries apart, would ever come in contact with each other and their willingness to build a multicultural family in a time when it was frowned upon. They leaned into each other as the world wanted to pull them apart. We faced many injustices in our family, individually and as a whole. It seemed no one could understand our family's genetic makeup, most of all me.

When I was young, there was only one thing I wanted to be: blond. Oh, to be a blond-haired, blue-eyed, stick-skinny girl. This was my life dream, to transform into what I assumed society deemed as beautiful and worthy. I had to come to terms with the fact that I would never fit into the norm of any stereotype. I had to look inward for beauty and strength.

Walking through the hallway of my middle school, I endured narrow-minded, ugly comments. Mean boys called me "wetback" as they brushed their hands across my shoulder blades; they would run up behind me and yell, "Pesos, pesos." Their ultimate goal was to make me feel othered, like I did not belong, but they only fueled my flames. I held my books tightly to my chest and walked quickly to my classroom, where I would work hard to be the best student in the room, to prove my intelligence to my classmates and myself.

Those callous comments couldn't cut deep enough to damage me, for I already knew my worth. Inside, I could hear my mother's voice over theirs: *The most beautiful girl in the world, princess of my life.* My mother's daily words of affirmation bolstered my self-confidence and sense of belonging. The unconditional love I received from her gave me an incalculable value.

Looking back, I am thankful for those mean middle school boys, for their insults trained my mind to drown out noise. They gave me the grit I would need to learn how to focus on what I knew to be true. I was forced to believe the words of my mother; it was believe her or internalize their hate.

The love of my parents is the bedrock my life was built upon. With age comes wisdom and greater observational skills. The older I become, the more I realize that most homes are full of chaos. My millennial generation is spinning its wheels to break cycles of intergenerational trauma.

Unbelievably, I am the product of what must be the first woman in history to break every cycle that came before her. Without a therapist, Instagram, or a parenting guru to follow, my mother made the intentional decision to love me, protect me from danger, and never say a coarse word about me or my body.

Looking back on my childhood, I imagine myself on a swing in my front yard. My parents are pushing me back and forth between them. Each emanating love and safety toward me, a slow and steady wavering between these two concepts secured my whole being.

Our parents did everything humanly possible for me and my two brothers to know that we were simultaniously loved and safe in their care.

My favorite quote by Maya Angelou embodies my perspective on this perfectly: "I've learned that people will forget what you said, people will forget what you did, but people will never forget how you made them feel." Even if I can't remember every detail or word spoken to me as a child, I always knew I was always loved.

They told us on numerous occasions, "You will have what you need, but you won't always get what you want." With my parents being frustratingly frugal, at times I felt like this was an affront to their love. All I wanted was a shirt that said Abercrombie and Fitch in bold letters, to be like the Britneys and Haleys of my class. But I had to wear my brother's hand-me-down husky Wranglers and shirts from Kmart.

My parents were playing the long game; they were smart. Not only were they thinking of their future; they were preparing me for mine. I learned young how to shop at a thrift store to find a good deal, and as an adult, I try to buy clothes only at consignment sales. When I was a teenager, if there was something I wanted, perhaps a North Face jacket or an iPod, I had to work an actual job to earn the money to buy it. It was like I grew up with Dave Ramsey as a dad, minus the radio talk show.

With their unending support and our pastoral childhood, my brothers and I thrived in the world.

Now, of course, nothing is perfect, and there were bumps along the way. But in our family we can all say our home was an idyllic launching point for the "real world." It feels like we were the last kiddos to be raised on a farm, and with coffee and tobacco farmers present in our family tree, we were built to be outside. All of us have an innate desire to be in nature, hands in the dirt.

We are also the first generation of kids who all graduated from college, even though none of our parents or grandparents did. It was understood that we would perform well in school and go to college. There was no pressure from family or even the school system at that time; it was just the natural progression of life in the early 2000s.

My parents lovingly paid for me to attend college, a debt they never intended for me to pay back. I am forever grateful for that opportunity. It allowed me growth and introspection in a crucial developmental time. I attended a small Christian liberal arts school called Gardner-Webb University. It was there that I found my soul sisters, life teachers, and education. It was within that tiny one-stoplight town that I experienced true community for the first time. This would also be the place where I would meet my husband.

This is our "meet cute," a story that had been four years in the making. Unlike many college sweethearts, we were gifted with four years of platonic friendship before our relationship bloomed into love.

One day during my senior year of college, I was doing homework at the local coffee shop. I heard the doorbell toll, and one of my old friends breezed through. Joseph had previously graduated from GWU and spent a year traveling abroad in Australia. He looked older to me, seasoned with sun: hair blond and skin tanned. He was happy to be back in the coffee shop, and friends ran to greet him. I was observing a homecoming; he was the king of this court. Once the crowd subsided, I pushed back my chair and approached him.

I knew I could wait for the others to move on because I was the reason he was here. A few weeks previous he had messaged me on Facebook to let me know he was coming back to the States and back to campus. We made a plan to meet at the coffee shop to catch up on life. It had been a year and a half since we had seen each other. When our eyes connected as we walked toward each other, our faces froze into permanent smiles. We embraced in a tight hug, and when he released me, I was shaking. He was too.

We were laughing and giggling with joy, not even speaking words, full of the happiness that comes from a heart reunion. We sat at my study table and talked for hours. Time passed, people walked around us, and the doorbell jingled, but I was unaware of any of it. I was in a state of flow, captured by green hazel eyes, hearing stories about kangaroos stealing loaves of bread and life as an Aussie mango farmer. I blinked and it was dark outside. The coffee shop was closing, so we continued to hang out at my off-campus house.

We sat on a couch in my room, next to a bookshelf. On that shelf was a little basket of *chunches*, random objects I had collected over my college life. A coin from Guatemala, a seashell, and a green stretchy slingshot frog. I picked up the frog and held it out for Joseph to see. I asked him, "Do you remember this?" He was confused and shook his head.

On the first weekend of my freshman year of college, I went on a campus ministry retreat at the Ridgecrest Conference Center. This was an opportunity to discover various groups on campus, a way to connect and make friends, a jump start to my new social life. I carpooled with strangers for the first time, quiet with unknown anticipation. We all exited our respective vehicles to be greeted by upper level students. The crowd parted and I saw him.

The most handsome man I had ever seen. He was tall, like an NBA player. Arms long and lean. His hair was also long and blond like a surfer dude, half up in a hair tie. I distinctly remember thinking to myself, *I wonder if that guy would marry me.*

I walked straight up to him, with no fear or shame, reading that his high-school-era shirt said "Seymour Eagles." I had never seen that curious word spelled out before and said, "Ha, more like see-more-butts." I thought this joke was hilarious and displayed how cute and witty I was. I thought I was flirting with my future husband, and he was appalled. This upperclassman promptly dismissed my joke and said, "Yeah, like I've never heard that before."

I was shut down and embarrassed. How could I have made such a fool of myself in the first ten seconds of the weekend? We were all corralled into an auditorium to begin the weekend's festivities. I was in the center of a row, in the middle of the room, all alone. Observing the ebb and flow of the people, I noticed the same upperclassman take up one of the doorways with his broad shoulders. I was glad to see his face again, as it was pleasant to look at. His jawline and the silhouette of his nose looked like a Greek god that had been chiseled out of marble.

I watched as he pulled something green out of his pocket, lifted it in the air, and flicked it out randomly into the room. In slow motion, a green frog flew across the air and landed by my feet. With speed and discretion, I reached down and picked it up. It was a soft, rubbery toy, probably ordered in mass from Oriental Trading Company. I put the frog in my purse, and the weekend began.

After the retreat came to an end, we had to carpool back to campus. I was the luckiest girl in the world, as again I ended up riding in the same vehicle as that upperclassman. In this car ride, the driver almost wrecked the car, which became a scary situation. I deeply needed to make a joke to relieve the pain and fear of the death-defying driver. I could not stop myself from blabbing. I said, "Whew, good thing you didn't wreck, can't mess this up," as I pointed to my face. The look that the upperclassman gave me from the passenger seat could have cut diamonds. It was the second idiotic thing I had said in front of him that weekend, severing any hope of a romantic future.

Somehow, my first asinine weekend meeting with Joseph set us up for four years of platonic friendship. What felt like the strongest attraction I had ever had to a face, disappeared. It was gone, and all that was left was a sweet friendship. I had a lot of growing up to do; my brain was busy learning how to function outside the safety of my hometown, amongst strangers from all over the world. Thank goodness, as time went on I learned to hone my frivolous comedic comments, to be used at appropriate times.

Joseph and I became friends slowly, he was compadres with everyone on campus, so it was easy for our paths to cross frequently. He was a Resident Advisor for a hall in his dorm, this meant he was in charge of about 30 guys, providing them with assistance with whatever came about. He went out of his way to plan fun and random activities, for whoever was around at the time.

Joseph had a huge fish tank in his room. He would take a carload of students to a local aquarium store to buy small feeder fish. They would bring them back to his dorm, and drop them in the tank where he had two carnivorous fish. The guys would cheer for their feeder fish, as the carnivorous fish tried to eat them; the person whose fish lasted the longest was the winner.

I remember being in his room with a bunch of students, and he opened a package of sugar wafer cookies. He would yell out random tasks, and the first person to accomplish said task would get a cookie. We all fought like dogs to win one little sugar wafer. Joseph sought out ways to make sure everyone was included in the fun, he knew these would be the memories we would all remember fondly.

In our years of on-campus friendship, and his time spent in Australia, we were able to grow in our prospective ways.

My parents' love story created a loving, safe place for me to grow, and they gave my siblings and me the tools we needed to thrive. I longed to create that kind of experience for my future husband and children.

In that meeting at the coffee shop, we were brought together as new people, unknowingly ready to embark on our life's great adventure.

2

MAY THE FOURTH BE WITH YOU

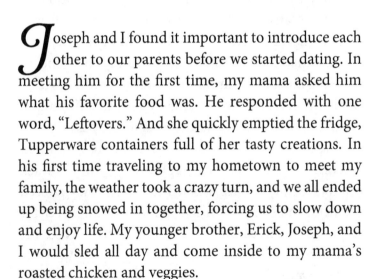

*J*oseph and I found it important to introduce each other to our parents before we started dating. In meeting him for the first time, my mama asked him what his favorite food was. He responded with one word, "Leftovers." And she quickly emptied the fridge, Tupperware containers full of her tasty creations. In his first time traveling to my hometown to meet my family, the weather took a crazy turn, and we all ended up being snowed in together, forcing us to slow down and enjoy life. My younger brother, Erick, Joseph, and I would sled all day and come inside to my mama's roasted chicken and veggies.

My parents were smitten with Joseph, and they recognized quickly that he was the one. They had been praying for my future husband since the day I was born. Their support of me in life gave me confidence, and their example of love proved to be worth waiting for. I never had to "look for love in all the wrong places." I did kiss a few frogs along the way, but nothing stuck around for long. When I brought Joseph home to meet my parents and they saw that his character was uniquely similar to my daddy's (hardworking, safe, and fun), they knew they were meeting their future son-in-law.

When I traveled to Seymour to meet Joseph's parents for the first time, they were watching women's basketball. For some reason, I blurted out, "Nothing is as exciting as women's basketball," in a highly sarcastic tone as I walked through the front door. Come to find out, they are die-hard University of Tennessee women's basketball fans. I had no idea about this team's legacy and had never heard of Pat Summit in my life, as I am an Atlantic Coast Conference girl and look good in Carolina blue. But Summit had over a thousand victories in her career as a coach, making her the winningest coach in NCAA history at the time of her passing.

Even though I said the worst thing possible when meeting Joseph's parents, replicating how I'd stuck my foot in my mouth when I met him, they adored me from the start. With mutual love and respect for all parties involved, Joseph and I felt ready to take the next step.

We were married on May 4, 2012. Yes, May the Fourth, Star Wars Day. We did not realize what a cultural phenomenon that day would eventually become, but we leaned into it and celebrated our love alongside *Star Wars* fans. Surrounded by our family and closest friends, we vowed to love each other in sickness and in health. We had no idea how quickly those promises would be put to the test.

We began our married life in our one-stoplight college town. We both worked on campus to have the school pay for our master's degrees. We had very little money, and we worked multiple jobs to keep us afloat. Joseph shoveled horse manure and sold coffee beans. I tutored kids and babysat. We eventually sold the car my parents gave me and became a one-car couple, which is abnormal in the Southeast where there is no public transportation. I joked that the only thing of financial significance I brought into our marriage was my REI Co-op membership, and I stand by that to this day.

We had a healthy start to our new life, surrounded by deep friendships in the town where we met. We were involved in a local church that catered to the ebb and flow of the college campus. I could have stayed in that safe and predictable environment forever, but as life goes on, it takes you to unexpected places.

After Joseph finished his MBA, he was asked by a former employer to consider moving back to East Tennessee to help open a new car dealership. This was a great opportunity, the field he knew he would work in once his education was complete. And it would put us in the same area code as his parents, and since Joseph is an only child, we knew this was the right move for us. I was not yet finished with my degree, but GWU made a special allowance for me to finish my program at a distance.

With the help of our friends, we packed a U-Haul and drove the winding roads west to Knoxville. I cried for the entirety of that three-hour drive. I blasted "Carolina in My Mind" by James Taylor over and over. I knew this move was our next step in life, but I grieved the loss of our steady college town. I was repeating a cycle the women in my family had created: my abuelita left behind Honduras for Costa Rica; my mother said, "Hasta luego, Costa Rica," and moved to the States; and I said good-bye to the Tar Heel State to become a Volunteer.

We settled into a little apartment and eventually brought home a puppy, as newlyweds have the habit of doing. We spent time with my in-laws, and I adjusted to my new state. I started substitute teaching while finishing my master's degree. I knew this would be my only way into a new school system. After completing my degree, I would be on the hunt for a school coun-selor position in any elementary school that would have me.

As fate would have it, I graduated from GWU in December 2014. I did not know it yet, but I was preg-nant as I walked across that stage. As I received my hard-earned diploma, there was a new life growing within me. My angel baby, whose existence would save my life, was right there with me, in every picture and with every smile of triumph. This degree that was seven years in the making would never be used, not in the typical and paid way you would think. Nevertheless, the time it took me to obtain this degree allowed me experiences of growth and community that would help carry me through the circumstances that were to come. Nothing was wasted.

3

WHAT IS A HEMATOLOGIST?

Hope: desire accompanied by expectation of or belief in fulfillment; to want something to happen or to be true, and usually have a good reason to think it might.

On January 3, 2015, I took a pregnancy test, and as I imagined, it was positive. I screamed this news at Joseph as he took a bite of a pork rind: "Hey, it's positive, we are pregnant!"

Through a chaotic choking and gasping for air, he finally let out a yelp of glee. We hugged and squealed with joy in the kitchen.

We threw our "Five-Year Plan" out the window and started making phone calls. All the parents, grand-parents, siblings, and close friends cheered across FaceTime calls with us as we shared the great news.

WHAT IS A HEMATOLOGIST?

On January 12, I went to the local birthing center where I met a wonderful midwife. I planned to have a natural water birth, with the guidance of a doula and midwife. I wanted as little medical intervention as possible, in order to allow my body to do the thing it was created to accomplish. Again with the plans. To deliver at the birthing center, you had to be considered a "low-risk pregnancy." To prove this, there needed to be blood work done at the very first appointment. I gladly rolled up my sleeve, knowing my body was in the best condition it had ever been in. I had decided to cut sugar and gluten from my body the previous year, added in routine chiropractic care, and had been going to the gym frequently.

A few days later I had a phone call from the midwife. "We need you to come back in. There was a glitch in the system; your blood work came back so odd. There must have been a mistake." I was not ruffled by this in the slightest and headed back for another poke. They were able to get the results of this test quickly, yet again the results were only described as weird.

The birthing center did their due diligence with great kindness. They set me up with an appointment with a hematologist. I had never heard this word before, and a quick Google search taught me that this was a blood doctor. My mother-in-law traveled to this office building downtown with me, a great comfort as Joseph had to be at work.

I was walking into the unknown and feeling quite neutral about the situation. I had no assumptions about the reason for my blood work being "weird." I was a healthy twenty-six-year-old experiencing my first pregnancy. I studied the information board at the entrance to the medical center, looking for the name of the doctor I was about to see, and was taken aback when I saw, next to her name, Hematologist/Oncologist. I knew what the word *oncologist* meant; *Grey's Anatomy* was one of my favorite shows.

My spirit slightly weakened when I realized the nature of this doctor's work. The combination of her job titles meant that she was a blood cancer doctor, not just a blood doctor. Upon meeting her, I felt a quick connection to her, as she reminded me of my favorite TV doctor, Mindy Lahiri (from *The Mindy Project*.) I even said this aloud, and she casually responded with, "Oh, my brother went to school with Mindy at Dartmouth." This pop culture reference gave me a railing to hold on to at the beginning of a storm.

My new doctor went over my blood work with me. "Your complete blood count is abnormal and we believe either points to leukemia or mononucleosis." My heart fell through my stomach, and I could barely breathe. I had never wanted mono more in my life. Full of fear and confusion, how could I be facing the "kissing disease" or the cancer that Hollywood depicts as a death sentence?

At this point, I was early in my first trimester of pregnancy. The doctor told me that if this abnormality was leukemia, we would have to consider aborting the baby: there would be no way they could survive chemotherapy. I cried with Alma, and we held each other while this information rushed over us.

Joseph met me at home, and we sat on the couch and cried. I had to make the most terrible type of phone call: "Mama, Daddy, I might have leukemia and this baby may not make it." I continued to cry, and eventually, my phone rang. It was my doctor, calling to let me know that under the microscope, my blood did not seem to have cancer cells after all. To quote Mindy Lahiri, "Ex-squeeze me?" I'd spent a whole day in sorrow only to receive this information. The doctor helped me make another appointment to check my blood later on, just to be safe. After this roller coaster of emotions, I went to bed full of gratitude and relief that night.

On February 24 I had another appointment with the hematologist/oncologist, where I had more blood work evaluated. The doctor was as confused as we were, as my blood work did not give us enough information. She could tell us that my blood was being "reactive" to something, but she could not tell why. She would run a "flow cytometry test" and let us know the results.

The next day I had a call; my doctor was concerned by the latest test. I was scheduled for a bone marrow biopsy at the local hospital. This was the only way to get a better look into my blood-making factory, the marrow where all blood cells are made.

On March 4, when I was about twelve weeks pregnant, Joseph accompanied me to the hospital and as deep into the process of the day as he was allowed to go. After much paperwork, insurance forms, and changing into hospital garb, I found myself facedown on a table. The radiology room was full of metal and machines. I felt like I was inside a spaceship, thrust into a world I did not know. The air was cold in temperature but also in demeanor. Sharp edges, beeping, and covered faces brought me great discomfort; I did not feel safe.

I lay on my belly, my precious baby buried deep inside me. The doctor administered local anesthesia to my lower back. This was the only medical intervention available to me, as I was pregnant and could not be put under or given any pain medication. An older male nurse held my hand as the doctor began what can only be described as torture. I squeezed his hand with all my strength, transferring the pain I felt to him.

At first a small pinch, a cut, then the poke. A hollow needle forced through the back of my hip was used to extract marrow, blood, and a chip of bone. The feeling of marrow being cranked out of my hip was excruciating, a deep pressure, as there was no relief valve to displace the outgoing products. I was latched to my nurse's hand. I screamed. I moaned. I needed to writhe with pain but was told not to move.

I screamed, "Serenity now!" and prayed, "This too shall pass." I knew Joseph could hear me, and I hated that fact. For some reason, this radiology room had only one set of doors between us and the waiting room.

As I lay there on the table, with my insides being pulled out, I took great comfort from Jesus. I imagined Him on the cross, His suffering, taking on the sins of the world. I tried to be like Jesus in that moment, taking on this pain for my unborn child. I imagined that I was experiencing this momentary misery to secure a future for us both. I clung to hope in a way I had never experienced before; it was all I had.

On March 5, the day after my bone marrow biopsy, I received the dreaded news that yes, there was something amiss with my blood. I should have known there would be something found; they would not put a pregnant lady through such an ordeal if it was not necessary. My oncologist told me that I had a rare blood cancer. However, once again, more tests were needed with the biopsied marrow to find out the totality of the situation, and we just had to be patient. This type of testing is very complicated and takes time.

Soon after, I was able to see the most renowned high-risk obstetrician group in Knoxville. They were very kind to me and treated me like a "normal" pregnant woman. With comforting words and mannerisms, they taught us about our baby and all the basic information you receive at a prenatal appointment. They focused on the state of my pregnancy only through the lens of the OB-GYN world. This would be the last "normal" doctor's appointment of my life.

They asked if we wanted to have an early ultrasound, and at fifteen and a half weeks along, we jumped at the chance to see that orange-sized baby. Joseph's keen vision saw it before the ultrasound tech, and he screamed, "I see it! It's a boy!" What a feeling of joy we had at that moment. Knowing this new information gave me a sense of peace, and my posture shifted to one of openhandedness, with a deep belief that come what may, we would be okay.

We were quickly worked into seeing my oncologist, but she regretfully informed me that no hospital in Knoxville would be able to treat me should I need treatment while pregnant. This was shocking news to me because I wasn't sure what she even meant by treatment. And what did this say about the local hospitals that they could not help little ole me?

She suggested Vanderbilt in Nashville or Emory in Atlanta. My brain went into hyperspeed, and I wondered out loud, "Is there any way Wake Forest in Winston-Salem, North Carolina, could be an option?" I assumed that I needed to go to a hospital attached to a university for the best care, and Wake just happened to be a forty-five-minute drive from my parents' house.

My oncologist called me later that day. "Wake Forest has a unit that specializes in leukemia treatment; seems like it may be a perfect fit."

My oncologist tried to do several things to force blood in my body to behave. I was given a shot of Epogen to bring up my red blood cell count. I was also given a blood transfusion, to do the same. I was learning quickly about the different blood cells, the reds, the whites, and the platelets. Never the science girlie, I had to be quick on my feet to learn about how my body was supposed to work. All I could understand was that my white and red blood cells were reenacting *West Side Story* inside my bone marrow, and we needed the sharks and jets to get along for once.

4

The Worst Type of Phone Call

An unusually late winter storm occurred in Knoxville, which delayed the most important test result of my life from being finalized. In that time my pregnancy was able to move forward, without anyone knowing the true contents of my bone marrow. This weather delay allowed our baby boy to continue to grow; it pushed us into the second trimester, a life-saving weather snafu.

On March 21, 2015, I received the phone call that would change the course of my life forever. The final test results were in: I had acute myelomonocytic leukemia (AMML), a rare subtype of acute myeloid leukemia (AML).

These results were both good and bad. The good news was that AMML can be put into remission with chemotherapy, the bad news being that if not treated as soon as possible, it would be a death sentence.

As soon as I got off the phone with my oncologist, a nurse from Wake Forest called me. "Hello there, please pack a week's worth of clothes, keep it comfortable, bring books and house slippers." She was so calm about the whole thing, pragmatic in a healthy way, she gave me a sense of peace that calmed my heart for the next task on my list.

I hung up the phone, only to pick it up again to make the worst type of phone call. Over and over, I dialed the ones we had loved along the way.

"Hey friend, I am calling to let you know that I have cancer, and I wanted you to hear it from me first. I have leukemia and have to seek care in North Carolina. I don't know what is going to happen to me or our baby, but we have hope that everything is going to be okay. I love you. Please pray for me."

Joseph and I packed up some clothes, books, toiletries, and electronics. We dropped our dog at my in-laws and headed east to the land of the pines. We spent the night in my childhood home, the cozy feeling of cherished memories and love surrounding me. My paternal grandparents came down the mountain to see me; my dad had waited to tell them the entirety of the situation, for me to be able to tell them face-to-face.

I remember holding my nannie's hands as I told her the truth, that I had cancer. The confusion and fear streamed down her face; she tried to stifle her tears and agony, but I knew she was terrified for me.

As I held her hands, I noticed new wrinkles present, sunspots, and pronounced veins. All the tobacco she had primed, the quilts she had sewn, and the cakes she had made, all products of those hands. She lived a life of service to others, and that required her hands to be busy and constantly working.

I thought to myself, *This is what I want.*

I needed to survive what was coming my way so that one day I would look down and see weathered and worn hands, proof of a life long and well lived.

The next day my parents, Joseph, and I traveled to Wake Forest Baptist Medical Center, which in 2021 changed its name to Atrium Health Wake Forest Baptist, and for the remainder of this book, I will refer to it as Wake. We navigated the parking lot and eventually found our way to a small doctor's office. We waited patiently for my intake oncologist.

Dr. Howard entered the tiny office, and introductions began. She held the attention of the room with her confidence but also her kindness. She had a way of making me feel calm; I knew from the second we met that she would take care of me and my baby.

She took her time explaining what AML is and what is unique about my AMML subtype. She also explained that she had spent time as a pediatric doctor before she was an oncologist, which led her to have special consideration for me and my unborn baby.

There had never been, in history, a pregnant woman in her second trimester diagnosed with this type of leukemia. I was suddenly a unicorn, unnatural and unable to be understood. The oncologists at Wake did not know how to treat me, so they reached out to ten leukemia specialists around the country to ask for recommendations. They received ten different answers.

They contacted Dr. Elyse Cardonick, a high-risk OB-GYN who specializes in the treatment of women who are diagnosed with cancer while pregnant. This was a great resource, but even in their database, no one had been in my exact situation.

Dr. Howard explained that I had three options: I could abort the baby, start treatment immediately, and I would live. I could defer treatment until the baby was viable outside the womb, but on account of how aggressive AML is, I would die shortly after his birth. The last option was for me to start chemotherapy immediately and hope for the best. She then told me that I needed to make my decision quickly.

As I sat up on the examination table, tears poured down my face. I could not bear to look at my mama, but I could hear her sobs. I was a mere twenty-six years old, the same age that she'd been when she had me. I closed my eyes and prayed for guidance. I felt a knowing, deep in my being, that the only reason I'd found out that I had leukemia was because of my baby.

We watched my blood work change from "weird and possibly mono" to full-on AML. We caught it as early as humanly possible. I never even had a leukemia symptom. This same diagnosis found later in its progression is a worst-case scenario. The only reason I found out that I had cancer was because I'd had blood work done at the midwife center. I had to give my baby a chance; there must be a purpose in this chaos.

I opened my eyes; everyone was looking at me. I was the one who had to make the decision. I said aloud, with a shaky voice, "Let's start treatment. I have to give him a chance to live."

Dr. Howard explained how little research there was on babies exposed to chemotherapy in utero. There was a small chance he would have heart issues in life and stunted growth in his appendages. But these were just ideas, nothing concrete. The only mass number of statistics to refer to for this situation was the population of babies born exposed to opioids and recreational drugs. Looking back, this was a strange foreboding for the future of our family.

She told us that my oncologists and OB-GYN doctors would all work together as a team and would all respect my decision. In this conversation, I somehow recalled the confidence my lifetime had built up in me and made a request: "Moving forward, I need everyone to believe that this is going to work. That my baby and I will both make it through this."

Dr. Howard quickly reassured me, "Yes, everyone will be working from this mind-set." They would communicate every step of the way and make and adjust treatment plans that best suited me and the baby. I would need one big round of chemo, called induction. Then four "booster" rounds, called consolidation, to ensure that the leukemia was eradicated from my body forever.

5

DO IT TOGETHER SOMETIMES

~~~

Somehow I made it to my room on the sixth floor, which would be my home for the next month. I was pushed around the hospital whenever they prepared me for chemotherapy, another bone marrow biopsy, and a PICC line put in my arm. My room was a revolving door, oncologists and OB doctors alike. My room had two patients in it, and both needed care.

The oncologist whom I would see the most during treatment entered my room; his name was Dr. Powell. He presented as serious and highly distinguished, but I quickly realized he was a big sweetie. The type of grandpa who would take his grandkid to the park and then get ice cream just because it was a random Tuesday. He introduced himself and said they would begin chemotherapy that day. For some reason, my heart exploded toward him in despair. "Please, tomorrow marks seventeen weeks along for my baby. May we please wait until tomorrow. Let's give him one more day without chemo!" I begged, I pleaded, I was grasping for control. The world was spinning, my body was becoming a medical specimen, and I just wanted to protect my baby from the unknown for one more moment.

Until this point I had hardly processed the fact that I was about to put some of the most toxic poisons that exist into my body. I could not process that information. I only wanted one more day without it. And that precious man, Dr. Powell, saw my despair; he listened to the pleas of a mother-to-be; and he obliged. He gave me the gift of control in an out-of-control situation.

As we were getting situated in our room, we had our first visitor. It was another patient, my next-door neighbor, Luci. She was about twelve days ahead of me in treatment, with a slightly more aggressive form of AML. As unbelievable as this sounds, we already knew each other. We grew up on different sides of the same county line; her childhood home was only ten minutes from mine. We attended different schools but knew each other and were already Facebook friends.

Luci had recently found out that she was pregnant, and felt something was amiss. Travis, her husband, rushed her to the emergency room, where they learned two devastating things at the same time. She was having a miscarriage and she had leukemia. They sent her straight away to the sixth floor of the Cancer

Center at Wake. Twelve days later I show up, the same age, pregnant with a similar leukemia. Now, I'm not going to go all Erin Brockovich, but I always thought the order of these events was suspicious. I even asked one of my oncologists about this, and they responded with, "We have to focus all of our efforts to try to save your lives; we can't worry about how this came to be."

Luci, Travis, Joseph, and I leaned into each other. No matter how or why we were all there, we made the most of it. We were all the same age, in the same stage of life, and in desperate need of a reprieve from the world of cancer. God granted us the gift of community in the hospital, and we were all better for it.

I always felt a deep pain in my heart for Luci, because her loss shined a light on her leukemia, while the discovery of my baby exposed mine. I wasn't sure how much to talk about my baby, as I did not want to hurt her, knowing she was grieving this tremendous loss while fighting for her life.

A few days into my time at Wake, it came time for Luci to shave her head. In an act of solidarity, we threw a haircut party together. Joseph clipped my hair to about an inch short, while Travis shaved Luci's head clean. There was some power gained by doing this together. We laughed, and nurses came into the room to take pictures and cheer us on. Our old friend from Boiling Springs, Matt O had a saying about community that rang true in my head at this moment: "Do it together sometimes."

The gift of community with Travis and Luci reminded me of childhood weekends spent up on the mountain at my paternal grandparents' home. Nannie and Papa live near the city of Mount Airy, the real town that was fictionalized as Mayberry in *The Andy Griffith Show*. I was always confused by this, because Andy's show was usually playing at their house, the only acceptable television programming allowed, other than old Western movies. We had the opportunity to hop in the car and eat at The Snappy Lunch or get a haircut at Floyd's Barber Shop. I thought for sure I would run into Opie and Andy walking down the road to the fishing hole.

The people in that neck of the woods seemed to be just like the characters on the show. Kind and fully invested in each other's lives, salt of the earth, and bona fide provincial. There was not a bit of flashiness or pizzazz to anyone. That must be why Andy Griffith chose his hometown to be the archetype for his show, in the tumultuous time of the 1960s. Our nation needed something wholesome and decent to consume.

If you were to look up the word *rural* in the dictionary, you would see a picture of my grandparents' township. Farmland on every usable acre squeezed into every nook and cranny between mountain hollers and ridges. Everyone was a farmer on top of other trades. Even if you didn't have a farm, you worked on some neighbor's farm during the harvest season and on what they called "community work days." This is where the community would work for one family, to do whatever needed to be done, whether it was corn shucking, wheat thrashing, or cutting wood for the winter.

Many times, when we would spend the weekend with my grandparents, we would go to a relative's tobacco farm, for them to work and the grandkids to play. We would run all over the place, wild and free. Playing hide-and-seek in old tobacco curing barns, breathing in the scent of my childhood, the musty vanilla smell of the drying leaves, thick and crisp.

Some of my favorite memories are from this sacred era, witnessing people spend their extra time helping one another. In the present day, these same people continue their legacy of care. They lovingly share in the responsibility of watching after my grandparents, who are shuffling toward ninety years of age.

This rural community, this makeshift Mayberry, continues to have a special place in my heart. One of my greatest hopes is to participate in life with other families in this way, looking for ways to help each other in times of need.

6

*P*OSITIVE *V*IBES ONLY

*T*he day that I started chemotherapy, our baby was seventeen weeks along, exactly. As the nurse hung the ominous bag of poison, Joseph prayed aloud, "God, please protect this baby from any lasting effects of this chemotherapy. Allow it to do its job, and only that, to kill all the leukemia cells." We sat in silence as the nurse started the process—the salty and cold push of saline through my PICC line, followed by the chemo connection. She pressed buttons on the infusion pump so it would release the perfect amount of cytarabine that was needed for my exact height and weight. I was given cytarabine for seven days, through a continuous drip.

A few hours later they brought in another bag of poison, daunorubicin. I was given this bright red chemo for three days, alongside the cytarabine.

My oncology team decided, for this round of chemo, to treat me the same as any other person with my diagnosis, to give me the same drugs given to anyone with AML. There was one goal: to get me into remission as soon as possible. If they could accomplish that, I had a much higher chance of surviving leukemia.

This "induction" period would last a month, the seven days of chemo, followed by a neutropenic state, and then the rise of all my numbers, to bring my body back to normal. The point of this chemotherapy was to kill every leukemia cell in my body. The difficulty was that there was no way to target just cancerous cells; they had to kill everything. This chemo had a momentary yet detrimental effect on all the red and white blood cells as well as the platelets in my body.

I would dip into neutropenia for about a week. In that week, my body would lose the ability to fight any infection, virus, or disease. It would lose the ability to heal itself in any way. Since I was pregnant, we had to be careful to keep any potential germs away. My neutropenic protocol was strict: no touching mail or other humans. I had to wash my hands with the strongest antibacterial soap that exists; this soap is too strong to use anywhere other than your hands.

I could not eat anything unpasteurized, nor any fresh fruit, honey, sprouts, nuts, or black pepper. I could not be in the same room with fresh flowers. I could not shave my legs or clip my nails. I could not eat a berry with seeds on the outside. Did you know a strawberry is never clean? There are microscopic germs hiding behind each individual seed. Anything that was possibly contaminated was out of the question.

For one month, I would remain inside, restricted to the sixth floor of the hospital. We were very strict with visitors, even overly cautious since we had two patients to protect.

I wasn't researching any of this or looking at possible side effects for me or my baby. I wasn't thinking of what terrible thing could happen; no part of my brain or heart was stressed. I somehow remained calm in the most furious storm.

I must have been pulling strength from my maternal grandfather, my abuelito. Born in 1937 in the mountains of Costa Rica, his life was full of chaos and hardship, being forced to drop out of school in the third grade to work in the coffee fields. He eventually made his way into the capital city, started as a janitor at a hospital, and retired as the general manager. As technology and change swirled around him, he found a way to remain calm. His body exists in a neutral state of peace, and with the flicker of a happy thought, his face shifts to joy personified. His eyes disappear into deep crevices, his bottom row of teeth exposed as his underbite protrudes through his smile.

That calmness I inherited from my abuelito was an anchor for me. It gave me a peaceful, easy feeling that aided in my survival.

From the moment I was diagnosed with cancer, I knew that I had to control the narrative. Like a publicist for a Hollywood starlet, I would be the one to release information to the public about my situation. I had a deep fear that whenever someone heard the word *leukemia* about me, they would also automatically think of the word *death*. I knew how fast and furious the rumor mill could be in my hometown, so I had to do something.

As any millennial encountering a unique situation does, I started blogging. This was a great outlet for me to process my new reality and deliver information to the masses. I asked for prayer for our little family, and I described my hospital room and treatments, but mainly I wanted everyone to know that I was okay and would remain that way. Maybe it was another grasp for control in an out-of-control situation. But I needed to be the bearer of all news about myself.

I was bossy too. I asked people not to google my cancer diagnosis. Any quick search on the internet about AML will tell you it comes with a five-year life expectancy. But I was an outlier for this, since almost anyone who is diagnosed with AML is an old white man. Seeing as how I did not fit into any of those criteria as a twenty-six-year-old half-Latina woman, nothing on the internet would do anyone any good in understanding what was happening to me.

I put a poster on the outside of my door that read in big bold letters POSITIVE VIBES ONLY. And I meant it. I told my doctors and nurses to tell me only good things; I didn't want to hear about possible side effects or tragic outcomes. In those first seven days of chemo, I ignored the bags of poison dripping into my body. I snuggled therapy dogs, befriended my nurses, and watched too much television.

My ability to hope outweighed any normal inclination to fear. I could not allow the tiniest bit of negativity in; I had to protect my hope.

Joseph and I fully appreciated this time together, realizing that we were getting to spend a substantial amount of time together, even if it was confined to a hospital. We would watch *The Bachelor*, *Nashville*, and *Gilmore Girls* for hours. If I didn't feel like eating the hospital food for any given meal, Joseph would walk to grab me a cheeseburger from the nearby Wendy's. We made our new normal comfortable; we leaned into it.

I was told to walk laps in the hallway; lying in a hospital bed every day would quickly atrophy my muscles, and at some point shortly, my body would need to be able to push a baby out. Going for a walk was easier said than done, as I had to be connected to my IV pole, and I had to wear an N95 mask if I left the safety of my room. But once a day, Joseph and I would prepare for a journey out in the hallway. He would push my IV pole, which we lovely referred to as "Screech." We would walk around the hall, which made a big loop through the leukemia wing, and into an area where they treated other cancers. This was a trek through the highs and lows of humanity. You could walk by a doorway where a patient was taking their last breath, next to an old man crying out in pain, followed by nurses gossiping at their workstations. We would see family members arriving for the day, then later leaving to go home, hearts heavy.

No one seemed to be okay, except for us. We dwelled in a bubble of hope, with our baby at the center, keeping us afloat. We had a purpose greater than surviving leukemia and chemotherapy: the main character of our story was our baby.

Joseph and I would make up silly games as we walked around, knowing where to stand to get automatic doors to open at the exact right moment. We were on the lookout for our favorite nurses if they were assigned to different rooms than ours. We would spend time peering out of a wall of windows that overlooked a garden courtyard, dreaming of being outside in the fresh air, planning future gardens in our minds.

During my first chemo treatment, my body was happy. I never, not in my entire time receiving chemotherapy, struggled with nausea. Zofran was my best friend. Hollywood told me I would be in a constant state of emptying my stomach into one of those plastic pink tubs, but I never did. I never lost my appetite either—cytarabine dripping into me, cheeseburger in hand, comfort laughing at the antics of Lorelai and Rory Gilmore.

Our theory is that my pregnancy was keeping me going, in a supernatural way. I could not lose my appetite, for I had a baby to nurture. I did not have time or energy to waste on nausea. My body was busy keeping our baby safe. I wasn't thinking of myself, and I wasn't thinking of any negative outcome for our baby either.

All I was thinking about was keeping our baby safe. I put every positive thought and prayer I could muster into loving him.

7

In Sickness and in Health

~⚬~

Every day was similar, starting with an early morning round by the oncology team. If Luci and I were together in one of our rooms, with our permission they addressed us at the same time, to avoid making Joseph and I return to our room for rounds. This shared-rounds-experience was odd for many reasons: most leukemia patients are stationary, existing only in their respective rooms, most are elderly, and don't desire friendship in their time at the Cancer Center. However, Luci and I were both twenty-six, and vibrant young women. We needed to create a new way of life to survive, we deeply needed each other, and if that meant shared rounds, all doctors obliged

I had daily visits from my OB team. They would come in midmorning and check our baby's heart rate.

This was the most comforting ritual, reminding us that our little guy was doing just fine, his heart rate steady.

Every night was the same too. My six-foot-four husband would turn the small couch in our room into a makeshift bed, which his feet hung off of no matter which way he lay. He never complained about this, not once. He would turn on an app that created white noise to drown out the crashing carts and slamming doors from the hallway. He would then turn on an audiobook in the hope that we would fall asleep quickly.

As a pregnant lady, being continuously pumped full of IV fluids, I had to urinate frequently. During the first night of this, I realized I could not go to the bathroom alone. I had to unplug Screech from the wall, but the plug did not want to come with it. I pulled with all my might and almost fell on the floor. I eventually made it to the bathroom doorway but was met with another obstacle, a tiny lip on the floor, that my IV pole wheels would not roll over. I was stuck. I called out to Joseph for help, and he rushed over, nervous that something was wrong. We laughed at the absurdity of it all; I was just trying to use the bathroom. From then on every single time I needed to use the bathroom, Joseph was right there, unplugging Screech and rolling it to and from the bathroom.

When we said our wedding vows, we had no idea "in sickness and in health" would come so quickly. I needed him every second, in every way. I was completely dependent on Joseph. He became my personal assistant, answering my calls and handling all the paperwork. Dealing with insurance was a part-time job for him, and it seemed as though he would have multiple insurance-related calls every day. He also kept up with every medication given to me, even catching a nurse dispensing the wrong pill to me in the middle of the night. Joseph encouraged me to walk every day and held my hand as we walked together. I could not have made it through any of this without his love and care.

We came up with little goals and challenges for our sanity and spirit. We clung to positivity and hope but had to be active in the pursuit of them. My favorite challenge was making our doctors laugh every day. We told ourselves that if we could make at least one doctor laugh every day, that meant we were doing okay. For the most part, we succeeded. Those doctors may have thought we were crazy, but we did not care. We had to do what was necessary to keep our spirits high.

My daddy taught me many things: how to work hard on the farm, how to help others in need, and how to live out being a person of faith. I watched him wake up early every day to read his Bible. And as many families, in the Bible Belt in the '90s, he had us in church every time the doors were open.

He also instilled in me an appreciation for comedy, which other than unconditional love was the finest gift he could've given me. Comedy has always been important to me; in another lifetime, I think I was meant to work in the writers' room for a sitcom. I keep up with whatever movies and shows Tina Fey and

Mindy Kaling have their hands in, observing the trends in female-led comedy. I continue to be fascinated by the construction of a joke—the syntax of arranging words and delivering them in the most humorous way possible.

This love of laughter, this gift given to me by my dad, carried me through what should have been a dark and depressing time. Humor was medicine for my soul: much like an antibiotic stops bacteria from growing, comedy stopped sadness from taking root. I could not afford to be sad; I had a baby to protect. My ability to lean toward whimsy went hand in hand with my capacity to have hope. I had to believe that the best possible outcome was in my future, and I would laugh my way there.

In my blogging, I asked friends to send me funny videos online to help keep our spirits up and help pass the time. And they delivered. I would log on to Facebook or Instagram and have dozens of funnies just waiting for us to consume. One friend in particular, Taylor, sent me at least one funny video every day, and he never stopped. To this day he still sends me things that make me chuckle.

In all the difficulties and hardships of life, I have found laughter to be the noun and verb I most appreciate. It is mercurial, shifting from an inner and almost secret vibration to an action outside your body with sounds and movement. It is a thing you do, alone and with others. You share it proudly with strangers in a movie theater; a collective effervescence.

Laughter became the gasoline I would pour onto the fire of hope in my heart.

After I finished my first round of chemo, I had another bone marrow biopsy, and the results were exactly what we hoped for: I was in remission! This was the blessing of a lifetime, an indicator that my bone marrow had been wiped clean. I had a few days in the hospital before my blood counts fell to zero.

8

No Time to Mourn

I can give you a definitive list of the two most difficult moments of my life thus far: first, when my
hematologist called me to confirm that I had AML and
would need treatment even though I was pregnant.
Second, the loss of my hair.

Here is some key information about me: at the
time of this occurrence, I was twenty-six years old and
I didn't wear makeup (I still don't; If you see me with
makeup on, I am most likely a guest at a wedding.)
I would rather run around town in my Vans tennis
shoes, yoga pants, and one of my many Dolly Parton
T-shirts than anything else. I have dressy clothes, but
they are for special occasions. My daily hair routine is
simple, and it usually ends up pulled back in a ponytail.

I tell you all of this to give you a baseline for how
I approach my outward appearance. In normal life
my clothes and hair are not a priority to me. Many

issues trump appearance for me, like community, love, good food, laughter, self-care, and YouTube videos of unlikely animal friendships. I tell you all this to help you understand that I thought my hair did not matter to me.

Walking into my first chemo treatment, there were rumblings about the percentage of people who lose their hair; I think it was about 99 percent. With my situation being so rare, having a baby along for the ride, I was not able to fully conceptualize the fact that my hair would fall out. My mind was in survival mode. During chemo I was doing everything I could to stay positive and strong. The loss of my hair was not a concern that I could spare any of my brain power to think about.

Two weeks earlier, I'd buzzed my hair with Luci next door as an act of solidarity and on a whim. It was fun. It was my choice.

On April 7, we received the most amazing news, that my bone marrow was empty of cancer cells. This is the date we celebrate every year; it is the day I was told that I was in remission. In the cancer world, remission is the best word you can hear. It means the cancer is removed from your body, and if you can remain in remission for five years, you get to hear the next best words: *cancer free.*

The next day, I woke up to hair covering my pillow and sheets. Even seeing my hair all over my pillow, it did not fully register with me that my head would have to be shaved. After breakfast, I noticed hair on the table where I ate; I pushed it away and tilted my head down. I ran my fingers through my hair and brought my hands to where I could see their contents. Locks of stick-straight hair filled my hands. I shook my hands to release the hair onto the floor and repeated the process. The outcome was the same. I knew what had to be done.

There were several medications scheduled to be administered through my IV, so it wasn't until later in the day that we could take care of my hair. I had several hours to think about shaving my head. It was difficult to be cognizant, mainly because I had no idea what to expect. I wasn't sure how to feel.

The nurse unhooked me from my machine and brought in a clipper set they have for this exact purpose. This is a set that cannot cut the skin because when you are neutropenic, you do not have the platelets to heal even the slightest nick. Joseph laid a sheet down on the floor with a stool on top of it. I decided not to be mentally present for this event. I put *Gilmore Girls* on the TV, in the hope that they would distract me from reality. For the first time in my life, they failed me. I ended up turning it off.

To this day I cannot fully express or comprehend the true emotions that I felt as I looked down to see my hair covering the floor and reached up to feel my naked head. The best that I can do is to say that I lost something that had always been a part of me. When it was finished, I walked to the only mirror in our room. I looked up at my reflection and felt a sense of peace. I liked the shape of my head, which I learned is the first thing people say to someone who just lost their hair, "Well, at least you have a nice-shaped head."

After we shaved Joseph's head, his act of solidarity with me, I was able to reflect upon the experience and the sense of loss I felt. I realized that even though I consider myself a low-maintenance woman, I also felt attached to my hair and the femininity that it brought to my life. As a person who likes to be mentally, and otherwise, prepared for things, I had to forgive myself for my lack of mental preparedness. I accepted the fact that I did not anticipate how difficult it would be.

Up until this point I had not experienced any negative side effects from the chemotherapy. But on day 16 of treatment, I suddenly saw a cancer patient in the mirror. A bald head seems to be the most obvious indicator of a cancer patient; it is like wearing a human billboard that says, "I have cancer!" I would never want to discredit any person who is bald, wants to be bald, or has a medical issue that causes them to be bald. I understand this is a look someone may want to embrace. But when it is not your choice, forced upon you by a toxic intake of drugs, it just hits differently.

I knew from a young age that I wanted to be a mother. After all, I had the most wonderful mother you can imagine, so I wanted to repeat the sound of joy that she gave me. I imagined my belly growing, shopping for maternity clothes, choosing dresses that hugged tight and showed off a baby bump. I wanted to have that "glow" people always describe; I wanted to be beautiful with the bounty of new life growing inside me. But this would never be my reality.

I quickly accepted that this was the journey I was on, and I'd better like it. There was no time to mourn what could have been; my reality was not based on looks or feelings. My reality was one goal: stay alive. Even though I clung to positivity and hope, I still heard rumblings in the hall, from rooms where my fellow leukemia brothers and sisters had once been, now empty.

It seems like the very next day, after my head was bald, and my mind had joined my heart in an equilibrium of understanding, I bottomed out.

First it was the fevers, then mouth sores. My body could not regulate itself; I shivered under a mountain of blankets. I had to drink Muscle Milk to get nutrients to my baby, and with my mouth full of sores, I could not chew any food. I felt outside my body, looking down on it, like I was watching a made-for-TV movie about a woman who had leukemia while pregnant. Surely, this bald and shaking woman was not me.

I had blood cultures taken and antibiotics administered. I was surprised how quickly I was able to feel better. My time at the bottom of neutropenia, my body free of any white or red blood cells and platelets, lasted about three days. Once my numbers started to recover and rise, we all sighed a collective exhale of relief. My body was behaving exactly how it needed to.

In this time, we decided on a name for our baby: Louis. This is Joseph's middle name, and this pattern was a tradition from my father-in-law's side of the family. Having a name to pray for and talk about aided my heart; it gave me another reason to press on.

9

LONELY PORT PLACEMENT

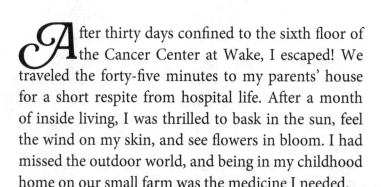

𝒜fter thirty days confined to the sixth floor of the Cancer Center at Wake, I escaped! We traveled the forty-five minutes to my parents' house for a short respite from hospital life. After a month of inside living, I was thrilled to bask in the sun, feel the wind on my skin, and see flowers in bloom. I had missed the outdoor world, and being in my childhood home on our small farm was the medicine I needed.

Joseph and my mama cooked for me all day; they used *The Cancer-Fighting Kitchen* by Rebecca Katz to fill my body full of nutrients, replenish what was taken, and store up for what was coming.

It was an easy role for my mother to take on: feeding me in this time of need. She had been constantly cooking for as long as I can remember. But I noticed the trend of her cooking more when it was needed.

Back when we were in high school, my older brother would bring a ragtag group of guys over in the afternoon. They would crowd around the kitchen counter, drooling as they patiently waited for a postschool meal. My mom would cook for them like they were kings; she knew these boys needed a hot meal and a safe space. She would become a surrogate mother for many, and she had extra love to give. For high school boys, to be loved and to be satiated with food were synonymous; no one left our house with an empty belly or a sad heart.

I learned from Mama that food was a comfort you could bring people; as a base need, it must be met before any other meaningful occurrence can take place. For those high school boys searching for belonging, and for me striving to survive, food was a balm for our souls.

My in-laws brought us our dog, Gus, all the way from Tennessee so I would have his comfort and company. I spent my days sitting in the sunroom, Gus on my lap, being served by my family, accepting their help and food as their declaration of love and support. I rested well. I traveled to the hospital a few times—there was always a check-in or another bone marrow biopsy to be had—but for a few days, I lived in outpatient bliss.

On May the Fourth, our third wedding anniversary, we made our way back to the hospital. I would have a port placed into my chest, instead of a PICC line in my arm, and start another round of chemotherapy.

I was told not to eat or drink anything before having my port put in, and as a pregnant lady, this was a difficult goal to accomplish. I was up till midnight the night before, eating and drinking water until the last possible minute.

I checked into radiology and waited with my family until my name was called. My intake nurse looked at me, down at her chart, put her arm around my shoulders, and kindly said, "You've got a lot going on."

My first thought was to laugh this comment off with a humorous quip. But when I noticed the honest look of concern in her eyes, I was brought to a harsh reality: I had learned how to cope with my condition. I had accepted my present life of receiving chemo while pregnant. However, I'd had months to work through a range of emotions to get me to that point; when I met a stranger, they were hearing about our story for the first time, and it was difficult for them to digest.

I had to remain calm and humble. I had to be patient as people discovered the difficulties we were experiencing. It gave me great hope in humanity that people were able to feel sympathy in a world full of negativity and self-centeredness. Our tiny family and our respective families of origin received such kindness at that time, a debt we will never be able to pay back.

I had to remain positive and joyful and give people the space they needed to take in what was our truth. I had to learn that when someone hears, "I am pregnant and fighting leukemia," they will need a moment to recover.

That sweet intake nurse led me through the process, and I ended up in another cold procedural room, with four walls I would never forget.

Everyone said, "Oh, you will love your port," and "Having a port is going to be such a lifesaver." A port is used to avoid accessing veins in your arms over and over; it gives the nurses an easy target for attaching you to the necessary equipment used for administering chemo, IV liquids, antibiotics, and blood products. No one explained how they put it in or the healing process. I tried to stay off the internet when it came to anything chemo/leukemia/pregnancy related in order to keep my heart and mind clear from false information and negativity; I never attempted a Google search on having a port placed in your chest. I had no idea what was coming.

They brought me into a sterile surgery room with a huge table in the middle. This is where I would lie for the procedure. The nurses and staff of this room were amazing; they even asked if there was any music I would like to listen to while they prepped me. I asked for Dave Matthews Band, and that was a comforting choice for me. Having a port put in requires a small flash of radiation X-ray to ensure the line is in the exact place it needs to be in my heart. I asked them to double the protective covering over Louis.

The staff for this procedural room had lots to prepare on and around me; they were worker bees in a hive, buzzing all around. Sticky heart monitors were stuck to my chest. Nubbins for extra oxygen. And, the strangest thing of all, a very cold patch of an unknown substance that was placed on my thigh to "ground me." I squealed from the cold and asked the nurse, "What are you grounding me for? What does this mean?" I was clueless.

She said that they needed to "ground" me so that I didn't catch on fire. Yes, fire. WebMD probably would have explained this to me. In this procedure the doctor cuts you open near your collarbone and then cauterizes the skin to be able to place the port. As the nurse explained electrical burns to me, my mind traveled back to my very first memory in life.

When I was five years old, my father was involved in a terrible accident at his place of work. An explosion of liquid sulfur threw his body thirty feet across a room and burned 25 percent of his body with third-degree burns. It was a miracle that he survived this accident, and as any near-death experience does, it forever shaped our family and how we loved each other. We had learned the secret of life, that it can all be over in an instant.

As I lay there on that operating table, I considered the fact that my daddy's life had been saved and his body healed in that same hospital twenty-one years earlier. I also wondered, *Why do I have to relearn this secret of life?*

The procedure went as well as it could have. My face was turned away and shielded to keep the area hygienic. I was covered in towels and a plastic sheet with various instruments strewn across my body. I became a table that day, a new talent discovered; I could always double as a table for doctors and nurses. The doctor numbed me to the max with local anesthesia, because, once again, since I was pregnant, I could not take any sedatives.

I couldn't feel physical pain during the procedure, but I was fully conscious and aware. I felt pressure and pulling on my chest. I smelled burning skin, a scent I pray never to breathe again. I was surrounded by humans, all busy with their individual tasks, but I had never felt so alone.

As I lay on the table, my body splayed to the hands of science and technology, all I could do was cry. The nurse stationed at my head wiped my tears as fast as they rolled out, a human connection I needed.

I had been holding it all together so well up until this point. But in that sterile room, my humanity caught up to my hope. Every tug of skin and pressure from my chest released some pent-up feeling. I was being cut open in every way, my physical and emotional body spread out, available for trampling.

For the first time, I felt alone. Either my sweet husband or parents were always by my side, but for this section of the journey, it was just me. Me and that precious baby. Even though I was falling apart on that table, I still needed to hold it together for Louis.

Wake Forest is a teaching hospital. Whenever I saw a doctor, there was a line of students in various years of their programs in the room. For the port placement, I was assigned a doctor whom I had never met before; we were briefly introduced in the holding bay right before the procedure.

Since I had my face turned away from the port sight, I never saw the doctor's face again or the student he had observing the procedure. At first, the whole thing seemed very impersonal; I was fully awake and conscious, and the doctor only talked to the student. I knew this was a teaching moment, but I was still perturbed. The doctor was going over every little detail of what, why, and how he was maneuvering. I was frustrated because I wanted him to tell me what he was doing. Then I had an epiphany, and I thought, *This doctor is not only helping me; he is contributing to the future patients whom this student will inevitably help.* I was a cog in the wheel of the future of medicine. This helped give meaning to the madness for me.

When the port was in place, I was rolled up to my new room, on the same floor we had previously lived on. It was comforting to be back on the sixth floor; we loved seeing our nurses. My parents and Joseph were already in our room, and Jimmy John's had just delivered my lunch (I hadn't eaten in about thirteen hours). I had tunnel vision, all I could focus on was eating, and I had no strength to speak. I remember my dad trying to talk to me, and I just looked up at him, unable to speak. Emotional and physical exhaustion was stronger than my will to be polite.

As the lidocaine wore off, I began to feel the pain, a constant ache that worsened as I made any movement. I had a "double-port," so there were two access points if I needed multiple IV lines. A port is placed under the surface of the skin, creating a small mountain range in the middle of your chest. Your body has to adapt to it; skin stretches over the bumps and tactile points. It feels so tight, like any movement might break it free from under your skin. There are three tiny raised dots on the furthest edge of each access point; this way a nurse knows exactly where to stick you with the access needle—much easier than having the veins in your arm poked over and over.

It took me a few hours to come to terms with the fact that I had undergone surgery. I felt groggy from the emotional toll, the releasing of tears during the process. My body did not have time to process this new addition and change. It was time for more chemotherapy.

10

BEST-CASE SCENARIO

The first day of healing from my port being placed was really difficult. Joseph prayed over the bag of chemo, that Louis's body would be protected from harm; he was twenty-three weeks along at this point. As the chemo slowly dripped in, I tried to limit the movement of the upper right side of my body. Even the smallest movement of my body seemed to affect the area around my port, a constant pulling. Even the liquid-filled IV line seemed to pull down on the incision site. It was as though I was realizing for the first time that my whole body was connected.

As the week went on, the pain lessened, proving how well our bodies can adapt. Joseph was vigilant; he had to help me every step of the way that week as my IV pole was too heavy and difficult to maneuver.

This chemo was also difficult to maneuver. I would need four booster treatments, and this was number one. I had six servings/bags/doses of a high dose of cytarabine. Each dose ran for three hours, unlike the previous cytarabine, which was a continuous twenty-four-hour cycle. My doctors searched to find another doctor in the country who had worked with a patient in my condition, trying to find a model of how to proceed with my dosage of chemo.

They were not successful, as there had never been anyone to walk this exact path before me. Each doctor they talked to had a different opinion on what to do. I was blessed to have a set of oncologists who considered all options and how they would affect both Louis and myself. They presented us with a "best-case scenario" that we all felt comfortable with.

This round of chemo was the lowest dose of cytarabine they could give, which they normally would not administer to patients with my prognosis. However, it was less harsh for Louis, and my leukemia cells had responded so well to induction chemo, that the doctors did not feel that this was a compromise to my health. The downside of this chemo is you have eye drops administered every two hours for the duration of the six days even while you are sleeping. Meaning I only had two hours of sleep at a time for the entire week.

For the first and second booster treatments, we maintained a predictable life. I would be inpatient for a week of chemo, and then go back to my parents' house while we waited for my numbers to drop. Once I was neutropenic again, we would check back into the hospital for a week.

Because I was pregnant, the doctors wanted me to be in the hospital whenever I had no immune system. This way they could have eyes on me at all times, nurses ready to administer antibiotics or blood products as needed. There was an antibiotic that I needed to take, but it would cause Louis's adult teeth to be discolored, so I had to take an alternate that could only be administered via IV.

I was at peace with the process. We had a routine for bouncing in and out of the hospital. Joseph figured out how to pack and unpack our belongings quickly. We had food plans: once I grew tired of hospital food, Joseph and my parents made sure I had good things to eat, especially my Mama's lasagna.

The OB doctors administered stress tests for Louis every day, a chance to hear his heartbeat and make sure I didn't have any contractions. Once during a stress test, my IV bag needed to be replaced, and the machine's alarm beeped loudly to make the nurses aware. At that exact moment, Louis's heartbeat jumped up as this loud noise startled him. The OB said it was surprising that he was this reactive at twenty-eight weeks, but it showed that his brain was working and able to react quickly. I remember smiling, hand on my belly, thinking, *He gave us a little sign that he is okay.* He must have known what I needed.

We also had extra visits to the high-risk OB-GYN office at this time. We were able to have many ultrasound growth scans and checks. Each time, we were reassured that he was growing at exactly the right rate for his age. We also could see that there was a correct amount of fluid in my placenta, letting us know Louis was getting what he needed nutritionally. These were my favorite days, as we collected sonogram pictures like Pokemon cards. I would sit and stare at his little profile, fingers, and legs for hours.

I always looked forward to my therapy dog visits as well. They helped heal my heart from missing my dog, Gus. One of the reasons why we had a hypoallergenic Goldendoodle was I had dreams of training him to be a therapy dog in the school counseling setting. It was surprising to suddenly be the one who needed the love of a therapy dog. I learned quickly that it wasn't just the animals who brought care; it was their owners who spoke kind words to me and listened as I told them our unique story. They may have been volunteers at the hospital, but their impact on me was as lasting as that of the paid doctors and nurses.

During this time there was an important meeting that needed to take place. One where all of my oncologists and OB-GYN doctors would meet to discuss our situation and make a plan. We were on pins and needles waiting to see what they would decide.

Everyone agreed that there would be a tipping point for Louis, where his body would be more viable outside my body than inside me and receiving chemo. The question was, "When would be the best time to induce me in labor?" The two main components to consider were the small window of time that was needed for my booster chemos to be the most effective and the right time amid the chemo for me to take a break to deliver him.

Would it be better for a baby to be delivered at twenty-eight weeks or be exposed to more chemo? No one knew the true answer to this question, but the doctors made a treatment and delivery plan that we could all appreciate. Louis would endure two booster treatments, I would be induced at thirty-five weeks, and two weeks later, I would be back at Wake for the two remaining treatments.

They also decided to give me extra antibiotics during Louis's last chemo, an attempt to prevent me from becoming septic. In the time leading up to delivery, my body would need to be functioning as well as possible, and being septic would have been detrimental to both me and Louis.

I imagine all my doctors huddling up like a sports team, hands in the middle of a circle, and yelling out, "Let's go!"

Always excited to see my new friends, aka my nurses, they surprised me with a baby shower! Not a dry eye in the room as they brought in a cake, ice cream, and gift cards to all the big box baby stores. I was incredibly touched by their love and support.

In between these booster treatments, we were able to go out and about in the world. After living in the hospital for so long, being anywhere else felt like a vacation. Any food outside the hospital tasted like a gourmet, farm-to-table meal. Any bed outside the hospital felt like sleeping on a cloud.

We made one trip back to Knoxville, to check on our house and see family. We also arranged a "Baby Moon" at a Bed and Breakfast in Asheville, North Carolina. This was a "normal" thing that young, expecting couples get to do, and I was thrilled to have a tiny semblance of normalcy.

We also were able to visit with college friends for Memorial Day Weekend. This was the best medicine for me, being able to see old friends, laugh, and even swim in a pool. I remember hearing that it's beneficial for pregnant women to be in water, to relieve the pressure from the weight of the baby on your back. I was again thrilled to experience this "normal" thing, letting my body float in the water, amid this wild and crazy time.

During this time, we interacted with more humans than what was normal for our new status in life. I had to accept that people had a hard time knowing what to say to me during this time. There was an uncomfortable, awkward, purple elephant in the room that people felt obligated to comment on or ask about. Some chose not to say anything about it at all, and I appreciated that.

This was not the first time in my life that people didn't know how to talk to me about something; my outward appearance teeters between Latina and racially ambiguous. Throughout my life, people have asked me if I am Native American, Hawaiian, Korean, or Mexican. "What are you?" "Where are you from?"

I understand the awkward-question situation; I don't know a life without it.

Believe me when I say I have mastered describing my family tree in a one-breath statement, and I can do it with grace and poise. I know that as humans we are curious creatures, and I acknowledge that. I pray that I am the only person you will ever know about living in the pregnant-with-cancer world. It is not as fun here as I make it seem.

However, if you do meet a sparkling unicorn such as myself, please do not utter these words: "Has that chemotherapy messed up your baby?" If you are wondering, yes, more than one person asked me that, in those exact words. The true answer was, "I do not know." However, I held on to hope and a constant prayer that our baby would be unscathed from any lasting effects of this life-saving treatment.

During those two booster treatments, I remained strong. My body did not show any negative side effects from the chemotherapy. No nausea to speak of. When I was neutropenic, I had no fevers and no shaking under a mountain of blankets. My doctors were amazed by all of this. They speculated that my pregnancy hormones were having some positive effect on my body's response to chemo, and all I could think of was, *How many times can this baby save my life?*

11

THE BIRTH OF LOUIS

*A*s my belly grew and my hair lengthened, questions from people shifted from cancer to childbirth. Many people asked me, "What's the birth plan?" My answer remained, to the tune of the Bee Gees song "Stayin' Alive." That's it. I'm a simple kind of girl.

We checked into Forsyth Medical Center on August 3, around noon. Around eleven p.m. we began the process of induction, and my water broke at three a.m. on the Fourth. I didn't think I would be able to experience the "water-breaking" sensation, but I did!

I always loved the movie trope where a pregnant lady is hailing a taxi cab in New York, looks down to see a puddle of water, and yells at the taxi driver, "Get me to the nearest hospital!" I wanted that to happen to me.

I was lying down in a hospital bed (as usual for that year), and I called out to Joseph to wake up because I suddenly felt like I'd wet my pants. We called our nurse in, and she checked me to confirm. Half my dream came true: my water did break. Soon after this, our doula arrived, just as my contractions started up.

How to describe contractions ... For me it was a lot of back labor; it felt like a giant was crushing my lower back in his fist. Our doula, Erin, had me stand up to help Louis drop down using gravity. She rubbed my lower back, and Joseph helped me remain standing, swaying with me through the pain. The pain was becoming truly unbearable, and we called the nurse for the epidural. The time it took the crew to get in the room to administer the epidural seemed like a few hours; it was only fifteen minutes. Our doula helped us read each contraction; she taught us that each pain can be managed by envisioning it as having an end. Every contraction brought us closer to Louis and to the end of labor.

Two doctors came in to give me the epidural. Lucky me, this was another teaching experience, so it took a while, to say the least. I was given Pitocin while the team was trying to work out my epidural, and my body reacted very quickly. I went from 3.5 cm dilated to 8 cm dilated in thirty minutes. Louis dropped down so fast that his heart rate was forced to plummet. Our room was suddenly full of doctors; they put an oxygen mask on me and flipped me over to help Louis's heart recover. I had no idea what was going on as all I could feel was the pressure of contractions working against the epidural.

I then had about forty-five minutes of contractions with just Joseph and our doula there to work through the pressure with me. Our nurse checked in on us and discovered that I was ready to push. Again, our room was flooded with people: two doctors, our nurse, NICU nurses, my mom, and Joseph's mom. With all of this movement swirling around me, I didn't feel prepared to bring this baby into the world.

The doctors instructed me on how to push by feeling the pressure that accompanies contractions, which was still in my back and raging. I pushed on each contraction for two full hours. Between each contraction, I closed my eyes and focused on breathing, giving as much oxygen to my body as I could. For each push Joseph counted to ten for me so I would have a guide on how long each breath had to last. The doctors kept saying that I was doing a good job, and I agreed. I was working harder than I ever had in my life.

But they needed me to do an even better job, so they brought a full-length mirror into the room and placed it in front of me. Their expectation was that I could see what was happening each time I pushed. They wanted me to see Louis's head crown and be encouraged to continue pushing. I yelled at a doctor for the first time in my life: "Get that thing out of here!" I did not want to see what was being reflected to me; I only wanted to see my baby. After two hours, one of the doctors said they needed to help me because Louis's head was stuck under my pelvic bone. He was in the occiput posterior position, sometimes referred to as "sunny-side up." There was fear that Louis was moments away from going into distress. It was time to bring in the forceps.

I pushed six times while the doctor used the forceps, and nothing changed. They said I had one more chance to push, and if Louis didn't make it out, they would have to take me to the OR for an emergency C-section.

There was one thing that could not happen during this labor and delivery. I could not have a Cesarean birth. For the timing of my various booster chemotherapies to work, meaning they are successful at keeping me in remission and thus alive, I needed to be back at Wake Forest in two weeks. This would mean, four weeks after delivery I would be neutropenic and unable to heal from the incisions made to my abdomen and uterus. There was a lot on the line here; it was truly a life-and-death situation for both me and Louis.

My friend Ali had prayed the night before that I would experience supernatural strength during delivery, and I called on this prayer at this moment. I dug deep within myself, knowing the end was in sight—it had to be. My eyes were shut tight, so I did not see what was happening, but Joseph recalled later that the doctor looked like he was going to pull Louis's head off with that oversize pair of salad tongs.

All of a sudden, the clouds parted, the sun shined, and there he was. The most beautiful thing you have ever seen. We asked them to delay cutting the cord for two minutes so he could receive more blood from the placenta. We watched and waited those long two minutes, as they cleaned the goo out of his mouth and nose; his arms and legs experiencing the freedom of the air for the first time. Joseph cut the cord; then they brought him up to me. I will never forget that moment. Louis and his sweet preemie noises rasping on my chest.

Louis's skin was soft, and his body lacked muscle tone underneath, adding to the delicacy of his form. He was the human version of the Velveteen Rabbit. We cried over him. We loved him more than we could have ever expected. The past eight months of wonder disappeared as we saw the fullness of this miracle.

All of a sudden, a nurse scooped him up, and he was placed on a small station in preparation for the NICU. They could tell immediately from his breathing that he needed to get there as soon as possible. I could see the nurses examining him, stamping his feet in ink, and weighing him. I ached to jump out of the bed to be next to him, to have his little hand grasp one of my fingers. However, I was stuck. I had a partial third-degree tear, and it seemed like it took the doctor forever to repair me.

Joseph was able to go down to the NICU to see Louis and make sure he was okay. A couple of hours later, on the way to my recovery room, I was wheeled to the NICU. I was so excited to see Louis, but the second we turned into his little room, I almost passed out. I hadn't eaten in hours and had used more energy than ever. Nurses rushed into action to fan me, and bring me water, and Joseph covered my head with a cold, wet towel. I was brought back to a manageable state and rolled closer to Louis. He was hooked up to many monitors but seemed completely at peace.

We spent two days in a recovery room, learning how to care for my body in its wrecked state. We spent as much time in the NICU by Louis's side as we could. Trying to balance self-care with the desire to see Louis was difficult for me. However, knowing that I had to start pumping every three hours helped get me back in the hospital bed to rest and pump. Within two days of pumping, I began to produce colostrum. This was a huge relief, as no one had been able to tell me if the chemo would interfere with my ability to produce milk.

After two days, the doctors discharged me, and the NICU nurses made it so we could still sleep at the hospital in the parents' room next to the NICU. We stayed for two nights in the hospital, mainly camped out next to Louis. A place of refuge for us was the Ronald McDonald family room. This was a cozy and calm area for the families of NICU babies, with a full kitchen, easy-to-fix food, drinks, and a bathroom. The people who volunteer in this area are sweet as pie and know exactly what parents of NICU babies need: food and quiet.

Having a baby in the NICU is extremely difficult. Your first days with your baby are restricted by wires and monitors. You are in a foreign place, with no comforts of home. You have to remember to drink, eat, and use the bathroom. You have to remember to do these essential things because all of your energy is being poured over your child.

NICU nurses are amazing. They know how to care for the tiniest humans on Earth and their parents at the same time. They have to teach parents how to do everything. Any parent is met with fear and confusion at the birth of their first child, but add in an IV, heart monitors beeping, oxygen nubbins, and line leads hanging off in every direction, and it's enough to make anyone cry. It is not the sweet picture you imagine, of a glowing new mom, resting in her hospital bed holding a chubby little cherubim. Instead, it's like holding a five-pound explosive, ready to detonate with any wrong move.

The leads are so sensitive, but for good reason—they let the nurses know if there is a problem—but for mom and dad, it is a nightmare. Any movement can cause a lead to jiggle and possibly send an alarm to the monitor. These loud noises signal the arrival of an earnest nurse ready to save your baby's life. A NICU nurse floats into your tiny curtained room with grace and poise, their movements calculated and reassuring, proving they can solve any problem that may arise.

It was a strange experience for me, to go from being a patient in the hospital to a new mommy in the NICU. I was ever thankful for my support system at this time. I knew there was always my husband or a grandparent with Louis while I pumped and took care of my postpartum body. It was a relief to know Louis and I were not alone.

Each day in the NICU, Louis improved, slowly being weaned off oxygen. He was given a nasogastric tube to aid in milk delivery; preemies use up most of their energy just by trying to drink from a bottle. He had an IV of fluids to give him extra nutrition as well. On his last day there, he was hooked up to a light to help bring down his slightly elevated bilirubin levels. He stayed a total of six days in the NICU, which seemed like a true eternity.

Leaving the hospital with him was frightening. Were we ready to be on our own? Could we take care of this tiny human forever? When I laid him in the bassinet that first night, I do not think I slept a wink. I watched his face in fear, not knowing if he was breathing. I hovered my hand over his chest to feel the rise and fall of his breath.

We did not know what a gift Louis being in the NICU was until bedtime when he went right to sleep when we put him down. He had been put on a schedule of eating every three hours—a parting gift from the NICU nurses for tired parents, the insurance of a few hours of sleep.

Louis Tanner Laurent was born on August 4 at 11:20 a.m. He weighed five pounds and nine ounces, measuring eighteen inches long. We made it to thirty-five weeks and five days, making him just a month early. There was fear from all doctors involved that my body would go into preterm labor at any point in this process, which could have been detrimental. Imagine birthing a baby with no immune system or ability to stop bleeding. I am beyond thankful that this was not a circumstance I had to face.

The thing that we had hoped and prayed for happened: my body protected Louis, leaving him seemingly unscathed. Somehow, my placenta, my body, and God had created a shield around him, absorbing chemotherapy and antibiotics and allowing Louis to be insulated from harm.

Louis's birth was a signal for my heart; it gave me the strength to continue to hold on to hope. It was an accomplishment of the greatest proportions, reminding us that we could finish what we came to North Carolina to do.

12

MIND AND BODY EXHAUSTION

Two weeks after Louis was born I had another round of chemotherapy. This was booster number three out of four. The doctors hit me hard with a very high dose of chemo, as this was the first time Louis wasn't a factor in this complicated equation. There was a reason for such a quick turnaround after delivery: all the research on this type of AML found that four booster treatments administered within a short window of time lead to the smallest chance of relapse. Even though all my blood work and bone marrow depicted that there was no leukemia present, there could still have been minuscule, undetectable cells that had to be eradicated.

I kissed Louis good-bye, left him in the arms of my mom, and Joseph drove me back to the sixth floor of the cancer center. We checked in; then he set up the room and left me in the capable hands of my nurses. I was getting hooked up to my IVs, and a sinking feeling hit me like a ton of bricks. For the first time in months, I was completely alone.

We decided that Joseph would be the primary caregiver for Louis while I was in the hospital. Louis needed to bond with at least one of his parents in the third week of his life. We had made arrangements with dear friends to come spend the night with me in the hospital so that I wouldn't be alone. But when the first bag of high-dose cytarabine began its journey into my body, I was alone. I had to be the one to say a prayer over it.

As the nurse who administered the chemo left the room, tears began to fall on my face. For every previous regimen, Joseph was there holding my hand, and Louis was under the other, resting amid the chemoed chaos. The room was now empty, I was empty; I had never felt so alone.

This round of chemo was unlike anything I had experienced before. In the past, I somehow avoided almost all negative side effects, but this was no longer the case. This time, after every bag of chemo, a gigantic wave of fatigue would crash into me, knocking me down. It was mind and body exhaustion. It felt like I had flown to Spain, run with the bulls, and taken a red-eye back to crawl off the plane and take the GRE.

I also struggled to keep an appetite. I didn't have Joseph to run all over the place to find exactly what I wanted, no Wendy's cheeseburgers or Einstein Bros.

Bagels. All I had during the day was hospital food, and it looked less than appealing. I did not have the desire to eat, but I forced myself to take in calories because I knew that I needed my body to continue to produce milk. To successfully nurse Louis for at least the following year, it would be essential to pump milk every three hours, around the clock, to force my body to keep up with what would be the schedule of a newborn baby.

For as long as I can remember, I knew that I would nurse my children. I was proud of my mother for what she had endured: a Latina in rural America, in the '80s and '90s, when it was not in vogue to breastfeed. She proudly nursed her children, not a bottle in sight. I wanted to replicate that for a myriad of reasons: to offer the health benefits to Louis after his exposure to chemo, to have a special bonding time with him throughout the day, and to prove to everyone that it could be done. Nursing Louis felt like the most important thing in the world to me; I was determined to make it happen.

I cannot verify this, but I think my doctors thought I was crazy. They didn't understand why I would put my body through the stress of keeping up my supply. They were actively trying to save my life, and I was busy trying to wash pump parts in my hospital room sink. It is possible this endeavor was an attempt to gain control in an otherwise out-of-control situation, but I had my mind made up, and I was going to accomplish this feat.

I used my phone as a timer, pumping and dumping every three hours. My body was not responsive to the pump at first, but a friend suggested I look at photos of Louis while pumping to help my body behave. While this was helpful for my physical body, my heart was completely broken. Looking at pictures and videos of Louis sleeping on Joseph's chest sent me into a deep sadness. I needed to be with them; I wanted to jump out of my bed and run along the highway back to my parents' house. This was not the way a postpartum mother is supposed to feel. This is not the way a postpartum mother is supposed to live.

After each pumping session was over, I had to unhook from the hospital-grade pumping machine, get out of bed, unplug Screech the IV pole from the wall, and carry my pumping parts and bottles and IV pole to the bathroom. I would ever so carefully dump my milk down the drain. This milk was not the "liquid gold" you imagine; it was contaminated, full of the chemotherapy that was running through my veins.

I found a rhythm to these days. Pumping and dumping. Passing out from exhaustion. Cleaning the bottles and plastic attachments. It gave me a mission in the madness. During the day I was alone, but busy. I had chemo first thing in the morning, pumping every three hours, around the clock, and I had to have eye drops placed into my eyes every two hours, to prevent blindness from the chemo.

One day during this treatment, Joseph brought Louis to the hospital to see me. This was a risky shenanigan. Most people would frown upon bringing a three-week-old preemie baby into a hospital, but my body needed to hold him. I needed to see my baby, to look at his face.

Joseph's mom, Alma, was accompanying my boys on this day. At one point Joseph and Alma decided to go to the food court in the hospital for lunch, leaving me with a sleeping baby Louis in my arms. I relished this time, the normal experience of a new mom snuggling her baby. However, this moment was interrupted by the crashing wave of exhaustion from chemo.

I remember holding Louis and my mind started to shut down; I was losing control of my body. I felt like an "unfit" mother. I did not deserve to hold him. I was supposed to be his safe place, but I was suddenly a hazard. I truly feared I would drop him.

I felt like I was hanging off a cliff, about to fall, one finger releasing at a time, when all of a sudden the door opened. Joseph waltzed across the room none the wiser, took Louis from my almost limp arms, and I fell into a deep slumber.

During the evenings, one of our sweet friends, Sarah, would come to the hospital to spend the night. This was helpful in every way. She kept me company and kept my spirits high. Sarah was present, asking the most thoughtful questions, and never treated me like the "girl in the plastic bubble." She gave me the gift of human connection when I needed it most.

On the last day of this treatment, Joseph came to the hospital to pick me up. We packed up all of our belongings, and I begged him to speed home. I needed to get to my baby. I jumped out of the car the second he put it in park and ran inside. I held Louis in my arms for the rest of the day, the weight of his tiny body filling a hole in my heart.

For the next three weeks, we lived in a modified newborn cocoon of love. After consulting pharmacists and lactation consultants, there was only a forty-eight-hour window of time after my last chemo bag before I could nurse again. This was surprising to me, that chemo so strong would leave your body so quickly.

In the time that I was receiving chemo and unable to provide milk, we received donor milk for Louis from various friends. A subject found taboo by many, I experienced it as a beautiful blessing. Mothers taking exorbitant amounts of time and energy from their own families to provide nutrition for Louis—another debt I could never repay. My heart has so much gratitude for those who supported us at that time.

Joseph drove me frequently to the outpatient center at Wake. I needed various blood products at this time. Since I was no longer pregnant, I was able to have my week of neutropenia at my parents' house instead of the hospital. I took preventive antibiotics, rested all day, and had plenty of hands to help with Louis.

I turned into a couch potato out of necessity, only sitting up for nursing sessions. I was so fatigued that I had to pass him off for burping. I would nurse him on one breast, Joseph or my mom would burp him, pass him back, and repeat. I was suffering from exhaustion, and my body was depleted of the essential components required to exist. To this day, I cannot believe my body continued to produce milk while neutropenic. This phenomenon proved that my body would continue to protect Louis and make sure he had what he needed.

13

A NECESSARY INVESTMENT

In late September 2015, I checked into Wake Forest for the last time. We brought Louis with us so I could be near him for a few more hours. I needed to store up baby snuggles. I said my good-byes to my tiny family and began the last leg of my chemo journey. I started strong, knowing I had just spent three weeks with Louis and was only facing six days of chemo. After all I had been through, the light was at the end of the tunnel. I was about to start my new life as a mother, back in East Tennessee.

This was the same chemo regimen I had just endured, so I knew what was coming. It was like clockwork. Finish a bag of chemo and then pass out. Eye drops every two hours and pumping every three.

We made a plan for another friend to come and stay with me during the evenings, Lindsay. She is the kindest human you will ever meet and a nurse, so she was the perfect person to walk this last leg of the journey with me. She had to work during the day, so I was alone with my thoughts during and after chemo.

Even though my spirit started strong, it quickly became downtrodden. I did not want to be there. I was done with chemo, living in a hospital bed, the continuous interruptions by nurses, and crashing carts out in the hallway. I was exhausted beyond comparison. I could no longer pray. I could feel the prayers of my community holding me up, but it wasn't enough. My brain was closing in, no longer able to hold on to the hope I had believed in.

Joseph braved bringing a newborn through the hospital again so I could hold him; he knew I needed to see Louis. I needed to know why I was stuck in a hospital bed again while my baby was safe and sound forty-five minutes away.

Those moments were precious. I memorized every detail of Louis's face and hands. His little smiles and smirks melted my heart. Holding Louis injected me with hope again. It was the Gatorade stop in the middle of a marathon, the boost I needed to press on.

When my tiny family left, I was lost in agony. Left alone again, tears falling into my hospital-grade blanket. My hormones and emotions were a roller coaster, forced to a screeching halt as an earnest nurse came in to administer eye drops. The nurse gave me the gift of time, to gain composure, to dry my eyes, so they could accept the necessary medicine.

When my hospital grandpa, Dr. Powell, came in the next morning on rounds, he could see the dread on my face. He knew my light that had burned bright with hope was wavering. He pulled up a chair and shared his heart with me. His ability to connect to my humanness was life-giving.

He explained, "What you are doing is difficult, but a necessary investment. It is essential to take the time right now to be sure that you have a future." This time away from my family was the insurance I had to pay for a lifetime with them.

I chewed the fat of this idea, of investing in my future. I thought of what I knew of the term *investment*. My brain called on all that my paternal grandfather had taught me about this subject.

My papa, who was born in 1934, decided to become a plumber-electrician. I find this curious as he had lived much of his childhood without indoor plumbing or electricity. He saw the need for this work and created a business to fill that niche in his rural corner of Stokes County. He hypothesized that as the population grew, people would continue to build homes and there would be job security in that domain.

Another way he taught me about investing was with the actual stock market. When I was about twelve years old, I asked him about which companies he invested in and he took me to school. My plumbing investor of a grandpa pulled out a three-inch binder chock full of information about all of his stocks and bonds. By the time I left his house that day, I could tell you the difference between a 401K, a Roth IRA, and a certificate of deposit.

Papa was a forward thinker; he took time in the present to make plans for the future. As much as I loved living in the moment, I had to think of the future too. I had to take what I had learned all those years ago and apply it to my predicament.

I had to invest in this last round of chemo as my insurance plan for a future with my family.

I dug my heels in and finished what I came to do. I completed my last round of chemotherapy, and said, "Hasta la vista, baby," to the sixth floor of that hospital.

Joseph raced us home once again. The feeling of holding Louis was soul-encompassing. My angel baby who saved me was just grinning, the sweetest face you could ever see. I held him knowing he was worth it. All the pain and loneliness I felt in the hospital had been worth that moment. Our pregnancy and his start to life were as abnormal as humanly possible, but none of that mattered. We were both alive, a testament to hope.

We repeated the outpatient life for the last time: almost daily trips to the hospital for blood products, nursing Louis, and being fed yummy food by my mama. I experienced being neutropenic for the last time and made it through without complications.

Finally, on October 15, 2015, we loaded up our Toyota Prius and headed West on Interstate 40. We were welcomed home by my in-laws, Alma and

Richard, and Joseph's Aunt Jenny and Uncle Randy were there too. They put signs in the yard and balloons everywhere. Tears rolled down my cheeks at the beauty of it all.

Wasn't it wild? Two hundred and six days of life in and out of a hospital. Two hundred and six days of leukemia. All to be seemingly over in that car ride. The time had come to unpack our bags for the last time.

14

BLANK SLATE

Every morning, I opened the blinds in Louis's nursery. I held him tightly in my arms as he looked out at the trees and birds. I whispered, "This life is a gift; the world is a beautiful place for you to explore." I couldn't wait to show him just how amazing life could be. Every time I picked him up from his crib, I would say, "Mommy's here, and she loves you so very much."

I was happy to be alive, to be able to pick him up from his crib and hold him. I didn't want to put him down, ever. But a strange part of our situation was, we had not been home to "nest." I did not get the chance to slowly wash and put away baby clothes or decorate a nursery. I did not get to baby-proof our house. I had to do that a little bit at a time. I needed this slow activity, the unboxing of swings and strollers, the closet organization. All of this contributed to the gradual but necessary rebuilding of my body.

The muscles that I had spent twenty-six years building had disappeared. I lost them all. Complete atrophy. Cancer stole my muscles. My doctor told me, "A healthy person loses about 30 percent of their muscle mass after being inactive for two weeks." Let's count back to see how many weeks I was inactive. Seven months. That's twenty-eight weeks. In those twenty-eight weeks I grew a baby, labored, delivered, nursed, pumped, chemoed, antibioticed, bone-marrow biopsied, and was separated from my family. I walked when I felt like it, but sometimes walking to the bathroom was the most I could muster.

Post chemo, it was most apparent to me that my body had changed when I climbed downstairs. It was catastrophic. My legs shook, and I had to hold on to the railings for dear life. I knew my body was a total mess. But at the end of my treatments, I was so happy. I jumped into motherhood with cups of coffee and yoga pants. I was so happy to be alive, to have my son, and to be back in my home. Joseph went back to work. My mother-in-law helped with Louis so I could get our house in order. I fell into a typical mom routine, and I thrived off that. Grocery shopping, nap times, and dinner preparation.

Eventually, I joined a local gym, took my negative amount of muscle mass, and slowly began to build back. I took yoga classes with the older ladies; their bodies gave me the encouragement I needed to keep going. I would drop my sweet baby boy in the child care area and devote an hour to my body. It needed tender, loving care after what it had experienced.

This journey would take years, the building back of a lifetime of muscles. I referred to my body as a *tabula rasa*, a blank slate. My main objective was to be able to walk and hold Louis. And as he grew, so did my body. It was keeping up with his growth. I went from being weak in the knees to toting a twenty-pound one-year-old up and down the stairs.

I discovered how to exist in my new life day by day. I was a recovering cancer survivor, but I was also a new mom. My life was tiny, as it needed to be. I focused on taking care of Louis and healing my physical body; it was all I could muster at that time. I had to rebuild my life and eventually make sense of what our family had endured.

PART 2

THE AFTERMATH

15

A WORLD OF
SUSPENDED DISBELIEF

~∿

When I began the work of writing a memoir, I was lucky to have blog posts that I had written in real time, back in 2015, for reference. And it was important for me, the writer, to share how I made it through such a difficult circumstance. With time comes wisdom, and with hindsight being twenty-twenty, I now see those seven months clearly.

Most people who are diagnosed with cancer are going to have fear, stress, and trauma around the experience. My ability to hope outweighed any normal inclination to fear. My brain did not allow my thoughts to ponder any negativity at the time. I would venture to say, my brain was not protecting me; I think it was safeguarding Louis. I wasn't just a cancer patient; my body became a protective vessel, absorbing toxins and shielding Louis's body from harm. This included my brain's thoughts and my body's reaction to the chemo. I never once thought I was going to die; that did not even cross my mind. I knew in my heart that both Louis and I would survive. My brain gifted me with the ability to have hope over anything else.

The positive mind-set that I clung to kept my spirits high, but I speculate that I disassociated for much of the time. Thinking back, the main things I remember from my first month in the hospital are sweet and simple. I remember getting to hang out with Joseph all day every day, eating cheeseburgers and chocolate cake, and watching the TV show *Nashville*. Was I subconsciously coveting Connie Britton's hair? Most definitely. I know the high-stakes drama kept my brain busy; watching TV was a form of self-preservation.

I jumped into positivity and avoidance. Which is not sustainable for a lifetime, but for this extended traumatic experience, it was necessary. There are mountains of research on the negative effects of stressors on unborn babies; there is a real connection between what a pregnant mother experiences and how it passes on to her baby. My mind must have known this fact and did everything it could to ensure Louis was shielded from harm.

I experienced the most absurd paradox in that time. Outside of love, safety was my most treasured possession from my childhood and something I desired to give my own children. However, the first thing I ever did to Louis was put him in an unthinkable and dangerous position.

I was not a safe place to exist. It was dangerous. It was a risk. It was the Hail Mary football pass with the hope that both Louis and I would live.

It was an offering of poison to Louis or have no mother at all.

I have my own BC/AC system for keeping time. There is a notable "before cancer" and "after cancer" life timeline. I consider my "during cancer" experience to exist on a plane, above and beyond all other time frames. It was so otherworldly for me, so distant from any semblance of normal life, there are times I think it must have happened to someone else.

When I received the phone call, back in March of 2015, telling me that I had to seek treatment immediately for AML leukemia, I was sitting at our kitchen table. I can remember with accurate detail the grain in the wood of the table that my fingers were touching. I remember the nurse from Wake Forest telling me to pack enough clothes for a week; the fact that we ended up staying in North Carolina for seven months makes me chuckle at the underestimation of it all. I recall the rest of that day making the most awful phone calls of my life. Telling my precious parents that their princess had cancer and their new grandbaby was in danger. I remember the tears falling down my nannie's face as I told her about the leukemia.

I never took the time or brain space to imagine what my parents, grandparents, and siblings were feeling at that time. The ripple effects of cancer spread through family ecosystems like a plague; nightmares become reality, and it seems like things will never be the same.

I was living in a world of suspended disbelief. I never had a leukemia symptom; we caught it as early as humanly possible. I never once threw up from pregnancy nausea or chemo-induced nausea. I was happy, laughing with the nurses and doctors.

Our hospital room was a haven for our nurses; they would come in and cry, allowing their bodies to decompress; walking other patients to their eternal homes was a raw and taxing endeavor. We somehow created a symbiotic relationship: we radiated hope, giving them the courage to continue with their daily work, and they guided me through infections, blood culture tests, and mouth sores. They gave me the gift of friendship in a time when I desperately needed it.

One unexpected perk with the nurses: several of them shared with me that they were pregnant before they told anyone else. I was allowed to carry their secrets, which made my dreams come true: I was living the life of a character in *Grey's Anatomy*. These pregnant nurses felt a connection to me in my condition. We were in the same place and time, living a shared experience; only, one of us was forced to sleep in a hospital bed at night. Strangely enough, if a nurse was pregnant, they were not allowed to administer my chemotherapy, as it was too toxic to touch with a hazmat suit and gloves, yet it was being pumped into my body.

I did not see my circumstances as dire. I liked my new daily life of snuggling therapy dogs and binge-watching TV. I was thankful for this bonus time with my husband, knowing most adults living normal lives do not have the opportunity to spend seven months this closely with their spouse.

My naïveté was my saving grace.

After Louis was born and the chemotherapy finished, the doctors spoke frankly with me. They admitted that we surpassed all expectations; they did not know that Louis would be safe inside me. They described our situation as a true miracle, and I concur.

16

MY CANCER SHADOW

I drag cancer behind me, like a shadow made of lead. It's heavy and invisible. If I give it control, it can fully weigh me down, pushing me into a depth of despair. I can fear-spiral into oblivion, expecting leukemia symptoms to pop up at any moment. Did I bump into a chair to cause that bruise on my leg? Am I a normal amount tired or leukemia-level fatigued? I had a lingering cough last February; I was certain it was leukemia returning to ruin my life.

No one can see my cancer shadow, and you have to be very close to me to know the weight it puts on me. I mask the pain and fear with laughter and perfect teeth. When someone finds out that I had cancer, they usually say, "But you look so healthy!" Was I supposed to look sickly forever? On many occasions, in conversation with Joseph and me, a person will talk about me like I am not present, they will look at Joseph and comment about me, "Wow, she looks really good now." I have become an object for conversation, rarely invited to jump in and discuss myself. I have learned people rarely know what to say, to anyone, ever.

It is oddly polarizing both to hate a thing and to appreciate it. Looking in the mirror as the last nine years have rolled by, I have hated the scars left by my cancer treatment: PICC line, port scar, and bone marrow biopsy holes. My hair went from bald to mini afro, then, through the awkward grow-out stage, turning more gray by the second.

At the same time I can look in the mirror and marvel at my body: wow, look at the skin and bones that sustained me and a baby during treatment and then nursed a baby for twenty months! Both a gift and a curse, cancer certainly changed me. It had to, because if such a traumatic unfolding of events doesn't change you for the better, then it won. Cancer will never have the upper hand in my life.

I was left somehow both stronger and softer after cancer; learning that I could make it through the most difficult circumstance built me up, added to the understanding of myself, medicine, and God. A softness was added to my heart, as every wisp of wind feels like magic, every bird's chirp a symphony conducted for my pleasure. I see the world through the rose-colored glasses that are handed out whenever anyone is able to leave the cancer center on this side of heaven.

I refer to the bottom portion of my stomach, the part that was stretched out by pregnancy, as "Louis's old home." To this day, when I look in the mirror and see the soft curve of it, I only see a place of protection. If my mind starts to waver and ugly words start to creep in, I can humble myself with one look in the mirror, at the scar from my port in the middle of my chest.

Until my port was removed in August 2016, I had to deal with the discomfort of that lifesaving device. Not only did it stick out of the middle of my chest, an indicator that there was something amiss with my body, but it also hurt. If anything hit it in the slightest, even my own hand, there was a special kind of pain to endure. This pain was both inside and outside my body. If a certain little baby's head was crying and rolling around on me, I would be struck on the skin stretched over my port, the inside absorbing the shock, my brain flooded in pain.

I used to ruminate that leukemia would return, as it has a high rate of recurrence. This caused me to become obsessed with the concept of time. It seemed like my mortal enemy and my best friend. It was the mercurial concept that kept me up at night. I was the White Rabbit from *Alice in Wonderland*, chasing an idea, a desire for more. I wanted more time. I feared that leukemia would return and steal the capricious carrot that was always dangling, just out of reach.

The world was racing by me, and I was standing still. At times I would shift into a manic hyperspeed to try to find my place, an attempt to keep up with those around me. It seemed like no one else thought about it. I was the only person who knew the importance of time, believing it was the only measurement of success. Not money, accolades, or fancy cars. If you had time, you were rich, the most fortunate of us all.

In May 2022, MD Anderson Cancer Center released an article that sent me into a tailspin of anxiety, the likes of which I had never experienced. They were the first people to ever study the survivorship of young adult AML survivors. In the past, the only research on AML depicted a five-year survival rate, but that was because the average age of a person with AML was seventy-five. Those statistics did not apply to me, so they were easy to ignore. Anderson's findings for young adult survivors were much worse than I could have expected.

They found that one in ten would die within ten years of completing treatment. I did not like those odds. I lost my mind over this. I read and reread the data. I talked to anyone who would listen about it, seeking any wisdom I could garner. One friend told me I was easily one of the nine and would remain in the category of those who survive. They reminded me that I take my health seriously; I focus on nutrition and exercise to keep my body in tip-top condition. That gave me a little bit of peace.

Another friend I shared this with helped me push through from fear to ultimate truth. The cold, hard fact is this: all we are promised is today. The inevitability of death is certain for everyone. You and I are equals in this one moment, and we only have this one day to live.

Cancer gives and it takes. It steals and causes unimaginable pain. It does not discriminate and doesn't care if you are nice or healthy. I had an oncologist tell me, "You should have kicked more dogs because cancer seems to come after the kindest people."

At the end of the day there is a small part of me that is thankful for having had cancer, because now I know the secret to life: it can be over in an instant.

17

SURVIVOR'S GUILT

Survivor's guilt is ugly. It takes advantage of my miracle, the fact that I am alive, and uses it against me. I never once asked God, "Why did this happen to me?" I only ask, "Why did I survive? Why am I one of the few people who've had AML and lived to tell about it?"

Eventually, in August of 2016, when Luci was in her final days, in hospice, curled up with her puppy, I was at home holding my baby boy. When she slipped away, her battle complete, I lost more than a friend. She was my connection to our unique world. She lived with me in that other plane of existence, my coconspirator in all things cancer and hospital life. I can't remember what we did or what we talked about. We just shared our time and energy, not acknowledging the many elephants in the room. Our existence in each other's lives was a healing balm for our spirits.

Friendship in any circumstance is important and of the most value to me, but Luci was more. She was beside me in the wildest time of my life, and once she passed, I was broken. The guilt that I had survived and she didn't tortured my soul; why was I alive and she wasn't?

There was a point during our treatments when Luci had a secondary illness, and the doctors told us we could no longer be in the same room at the same time. We could not go near each other, because what she was dealing with was so contagious and dangerous, it could have been detrimental to me and Louis. This broke my heart and left me feeling alone. It was a foreshadowing of what was to come, but I couldn't see past the pain.

We shared a wall but couldn't even see each other. I know the doctors saw value in our kindred spirits, but they knew the risk was too high. Luci was two weeks ahead of me in treatment, and although she did eventually go into remission, her leukemia returned. She received a bone marrow transplant from her brother and experimental chemotherapy. She tried everything she could to beat it, but in the end, her body was exhausted and it was ready to be done.

The love of her mother and husband through her illness and beyond is a testament to how cancer affects more than just the patient. Cancer touches everyone involved, in varied and unexpected ways. They hold blood drives to honor her life and to celebrate the blood products she received during treatments. This is a legacy that will continue to help other blood cancer patients, indefinitely. I miss her; I wish she was here. I know we must still be connected, outside space and time.

18

ADULT FEMALE FRIENDSHIP

Whenen I was able to be back in Tennessee after treatment, it did not take long for me to realize I needed to find friends. The thing that all new moms need is a village; you know the old saying, "It takes a village to raise a child." My problem was, I was new to the area and did not have a clue how to find said village. I did have a great support system with my in-laws living forty-five minutes away, but the thing I desired and needed was women my age with young children to share in the highs and lows of everyday life.

I found this to be a very difficult time to maneuver through the world, trying to make connections with people and explaining what I was walking out of. I felt like I had to tell people immediately why I had such short hair and a big scar across my chest, much likely with an offhand joke about having had cancer. Of course, I made jokes; I was uncomfortable and insecure. Yes, many people want short hair, and I support that, but I did not choose anything about the way I looked.

Of course, I would make jokes to try to ease the pain of others. Hearing that someone had cancer is uncomfortable. I didn't want to scare people away, but I also needed them to know what I had just survived. Most people don't introduce themselves and trauma-dump in the same sentence. I felt codependent with my trauma, and I needed to explain it away quickly. People didn't know what to say, how to respond to me, or how to connect with me. It was like I had a gaping wound and I was asking strangers to help me, but they were ill equipped and uninformed.

What I desired was friends who knew me BC (before cancer) to live near me. To have the coziness that comes from established, safe friendships. But that was impossible; my college friends, my soul sisters and brothers, were like seeds thrown in the wind, landing all over the United States. My sweet husband watched me suffer through this time, about two years, knowing how much I needed friends but not having any way to help me. He knew how much my body and mind had gone through; he knew the value I would bring to someone in friendship too. One of my only friends during this time was a fellow Tennessee transplant, and she was the receptionist at my chiropractor. That's right, my only friend was someone who was paid to talk to me. We are still friends today, and I love that sunshine girl.

No one talks about this part of adulthood, the loneliness of moving to a new area post college and trying to establish new relationships. Knoxville was especially difficult because, oddly enough, it is such a wonderful city but almost everyone I met was from Knoxville, went to the University of Tennessee at Knoxville, married their college sweetheart, and stayed in Knoxville. This meant that everyone I met already had multiple circles of well-established friends.

Eventually, Joseph started working at a car dealership that his boss opened up while we were in North Carolina, out in Oak Ridge, about twenty minutes away from our house. We started going to a church in Oak Ridge that an acquaintance had told us about. We loved the pastors and people there, and I started getting connected with young moms. We decided to move to Oak Ridge since two of the main facets of our lives were there. I joined a women's Bible study and asked these wise women to pray for me to find friends. Little did I know, some of the people in that room would soon find their names on my emergency contact list.

I had been praying for friends for over two years, and looking back it seems like once we moved to Oak Ridge, there they were, just waiting for me. I knew that I had prayed for very specific things in my past, and I believe in a God who hears and cares. He had proved His care for me very clearly, and I needed to remember that truth. It wasn't the timing that I had expected, but once these friendships started and began to flourish, I could see the timeline did not matter. In those friendships, I found redemption for my lonely season; I needed to focus on taking care of my body and baby post-treatment. Once I was in a space to receive true friendship, new friends showed up and never left.

I am going to let you in on my favorite part of adult female friendship: it's the exchanging of bags full of random things. This is how it goes. I am meeting a friend at a playground with all of our kids; she has a grocery store bag with a set of jammies to hand down to my youngest, a book that I let her borrow last year, and a set of Dolly Parton drink coasters that she "just had to get me." In my bag for her, I have half a bushel of mandarin oranges, some Paw Patrol sheets, and a sweater I bought at Costco that did not fit but might work for her. It's an outward display of inward feeling; it's proof that your friend was thinking of you and wanting to share life with you.

There is no overabundance of friends in adult life, not that I can see anyway. I have learned that once you find your people, make the effort to show them you care—one voice message at a time, one reusable grocery bag at a time.

As the years have gone on, my friendship circle has widened. I realized the same formula that creates friendship in school is true for adult life too: you have to keep showing up to the same place over and over, and eventually, a connection will happen. For me it was church, going to the same building every Sunday, putting me in the same room at the same time, and enough times, for true connections to take place.

19

JUST BE THANKFUL AND DRINK THE PUNCH

As an Enneagram 7, I can find a silver lining in almost any situation; I have a deep need to avoid pain at any cost and an inner drive to have fun constantly. I enjoy introducing loved ones to new experiences. "Have you ever tried a Tim Tam Slam?" This is where you use the Australian-made cookie as a straw in a hot drink, melting the inside of said cookie and leaving you with the yummiest treat you will ever eat.

Throw being a cancer survivor into that mix, and you have an explosion of positivity and majestic unicorn energy. However, cancer brought difficulties to my life that are hard to spin to positives. It is easy to say, "Cancer was a gift that forced me to appreciate my life." That is true, and I can acknowledge that. But dragging that heavy cancer shadow through my life leads to inner turmoil as well as bumps and bruises that cannot be seen.

One of the first postcancer frustrations for me was when I needed to renew my driver's license. As long as I have had a license, I have had the heart symbol on it, representing that I wish to be an organ donor in the event of my death. But after having had cancer, I can no longer donate anything from my body; it is a tarnished good, unable to help anyone else.

In the past, I gave blood at any blood drive I was privy to, and I will never have that opportunity again. This is painful because I used so much donated blood and platelets during my treatment, and I would do anything to be able to renew the slightest bit of reserves for the Red Cross. My dad donates blood as often as physically possible in honor of me. I would like to ask you to do the same.

Baby showers have been one of the most triggering things for me over the last nine years. This may seem random, but it's real. It would have been too dangerous for me to have a baby shower, on account of exposure to germs, but I had a deep desire to have one. I hated leukemia for taking that from me. Every baby shower I attended AC (after cancer) added weight to the cancer shadow I dragged through the door behind me.

A baby shower is one of the sweetest events you can attend, full of laughter, snacks, and wisdom-filled ladies telling stories of their time as young mothers. The mom-to-be is always glowing and beautiful, wearing a pretty dress to accent a growing baby bump. For me, the base emotions of jealousy and frustration would be neck and neck. I was jealous that I didn't get to have my own and frustrated that cancer stole that opportunity. This would then turn into a shame spiral as I knew I was lucky to be alive, so I should just be thankful and drink the punch.

An uncomfortable situation I often find myself in is being among other women where they are recounting their pregnancies and birthing adventures. I can appreciate the nuance between different life experiences, and I enjoy hearing about other people's journeys. However, we feel pushed into a corner in these conversations, my shadow and I. I can't jump into dialogue because all I can share is the most insane birth story anyone has ever heard. It's somehow both a one-upper and a "Debbie Downer."

What am I to say, "You thought your eight-hour labor was hard? Try having leukemia! Did you get mastitis from nursing? Try pumping and dumping while on chemotherapy!" I would never actually say those things, but anything I can add to birth banter just doesn't fit in with anyone else's story. I would need a room full of women who were also pregnant with cancer for me to feel normal, and that situation would be next to impossible, as we are a rare unicorn breed. I am thankful to have friends now who know me and give me a smile in the middle of these conversations. In a room full of people, those closest to me know my heart and can acknowledge my elaborate history.

After a few years of processing my survival and contemplating the why and how of it all, I added a large photo to our wall. It is a photo of me from when I was in the hospital for my first round of chemo It's a silhouette, and I am smiling looking out a window, my hands cradling my belly. This is my reminder, my Ebenezer stone. This photo tells my family daily, "Remember what God brought us through. Do not give up hope."

PART 3

ADOPTION

20

BE PATIENT AND
HAVE HOPE

I was twenty-six years old when I had Louis. My doctors spoke with us many times over about birth control and how dangerous it would be for my weakened body to go through pregnancy anytime soon after my cancer treatment ended. They suggested we wait at least five years before trying to conceive again. I assured them that I would never become pregnant again; the fear of my bone marrow exploding with extra white blood cells as my pregnant body increased in blood volume was not an experience I wanted to have again.

When Joseph and I were engaged and dreaming of building our family together, we knew adoption was in our future. We both have a heart for children, having both worked in children's homes and youth groups in college.

When Louis was about eighteen months old, we started the adoption process. We wanted our children to be as close in age as possible, hopeful that they could be playmates and best friends for life. Because of my cancer history, we had to wait until I was two years away from treatment to be considered a "waiting family." Once we hit that two-year mark, our mountain of paperwork was finished, background checks done, CPR certification completed, and our website was live!

The way our adoption agency worked was almost like a one-way dating website: prospective birth moms could view our "lookbook" at our adoption agency, or read about us online, and decide if they wanted to meet us in person.

We went into this process openhanded and willing to accept any child into our family. We were open to any race, gender, or disability. We loved our little trio, but we knew we had the capacity and desire to love and care for another child, and we knew there was a need for adoptive families in our area and beyond. We worked hard on all of the paperwork and necessary red tape that comes with adoption; we thought we knew what we were getting into and the risks that came with the process. You could get a call in the middle of the night to rush to the hospital to bring home a baby, you could have to hop on a plane and travel to the other side of the country, or you could meet a birth mom who was only twelve weeks pregnant and walk beside her for the rest of her pregnancy in support. You could also match with a birth mom, paint a nursery, buy every outfit and pacifier on the shelf, and have the birth mom decide at the last minute that she wants to parent the child, which is her absolute right to do so.

We were prepared for whatever was coming our way; our previous experience in bringing home a baby taught us that we needed to be patient and have hope.

21

A MULTITUDE OF EMOTIONS

~~~

While I lived in the hospital, I walked daily laps around the hallway to try to maintain mobility and muscle. I had to pull myself up by my medical-grade grippy socks and get to stepping. As I walked the hall with my IV pole, Screech, I imagined myself as Cheryl Strayed in her memoir, *Wild*. I felt a kinship to her story of hiking the Pacific Coast Trail with no previous wilderness experience. I too was navigating a feral and unknown land; the dramatic terrain of cancer. Walking a little bit each day was exhausting but necessary, much like this beloved author's journey of self-discovery on the trail. I have often wondered if Strayed thought her life would be simple and full of ease after completing her transformative hike; I know I did.

I naively thought anything after beating cancer and bringing Louis home safe and sound would be easy. What could be harder? There wouldn't be any situation in the world that's harder than that. I endured bone marrow biopsies with no anesthesia. I am confident that is the most painful thing the human body can withstand and survive; I wish I was exaggerating. I thought I had climbed the greatest and only mountain in my life, descending away from cancer and into the ease that would be the rest of my life. Surely, I would be rewarded in life for having persevered; I even kept a positive attitude for most of the time. Where was my gold star of achievement?

I am woman enough to say, I was wrong. So wrong. I discovered that there is no easy way to bring a baby home for our family; we were built to endure beyond reasonable expectations. In March of 2018, we were told that a birth family saw our lookbook and wanted to meet us. We met in a public space with the social worker from our adoption agency. We knew we were the third couple to meet with Anna and Dustin, and it felt a little bit like speed dating. We all sat down, and they told us what stood out about us from our book: they liked that we did outdoorsy things and stayed active. They told us that they were expecting a boy and that they had picked out the name Jackson. We agreed that it was a lovely name. We didn't talk for very long, but as we were all leaving, Anna walked close to me and whispered in my ear that we would be hearing from them very soon.

A few days later we got the call that we matched! Anna and Dustin liked us so much, they chose us to be the parents of their unborn child. This was an overwhelming feeling. It was the first birth family we ever interacted with. We were excited, scared, and all the feelings in between. We called our families and celebrated, a new grandbaby for everyone to love. I got to work gathering baby clothes, diapers, and decor. A friend from church organized a baby shower for me, and even though I was very new to the community, lots of ladies showed up and showered me with sweet gifts and care. There was redemption in those acts of kindness for me.

In April I was able to go to an OB appointment with Anna and our social worker, Jane. I had been so excited to spend this time with Anna, to get to know her better, and to see little Jackson on the sonogram screen. We met in the waiting room, and immediately I knew something was off. I couldn't put my finger on it, but I had this sinking feeling in my gut. I was able to be in the room as the ultrasound technician showed us as much of Jackson as she could. Then we went back to the waiting area. Anna had several appointments in the OB's office that day, so I waited in the waiting room as she went back to be seen, accompanied by Jane.

I was alone in a hospital, which was not new to me, but this time I wasn't a patient. I was lonely and confused. I looked up at the television, and there was an episode of *House Hunters* playing; I watched out of sheer necessity. I needed something to occupy my mind. As I focused on the screen, I thought I recognized the couple; I was sure the people looking for a new home were a couple from my church. This would not be out of the ordinary since at that time HGTV's headquarters were in Knoxville. Watching people I knew on the TV screen helped ease my heart in that stressful unknown time. Later I told this couple about how they saved my worried soul, and they laughed and said they had never been on TV in their lives.

When Jane and Anna came back to the waiting room, Jane had an emergency call that she had to take. She then told us that she had to leave immediately. She told me that I could walk with Anna to a certain exit of the hospital and wait for another agency employee to pick her up. I was happy to oblige, and we started our trek through the hospital. Anna said she wanted to stop by the gift shop and look around.

As we walked in, I noticed the cashier heighten her awareness of the room. I started to browse the store, looking at odds and ends to give Anna space to do the same. All of a sudden I witnessed her bend over, grab a wallet that was for sale, and stuff it in her backpack. I was in shock. I felt sick to my stomach. I knew I had to make a quick decision: either be an accessory to a crime or tell the cashier what happened and most likely lose Jackson.

I walked up to Anna. "Did you accidentally drop a wallet from the store into your bag?" I was trying to give her an easy out.

She denied it. "I have a new wallet in my bag from a different store. It's from Justin's Boots. I can show you the receipt, but it's at home."

I was confused. I stayed beside her as she walked straight up to the cashier. She picked up a set of fingernail clippers and tweezers that were on the counter and asked the worker how much they cost.

As the cashier was looking it up, Anna said, "Wow, your eyes are so beautiful, I love the way you do your makeup." The cashier was an older lady, and this compliment took her completely off guard. She smiled a big grin and responded with the price of the clippers. Anna said she thought that the price was a little high, but she might come back and get them later. She put them back on the counter and walked out the door. I was stuck in space and time. I looked at the cashier, and she smiled at me. I then realized that I had watched Anna run a con.

I walked slowly out of the gift shop without saying a word. My heart was beating out of my chest, knowing that as the door closed behind me, I was officially an accessory to a crime. The complication here that is hard to explain is that I already felt like Jackson was my son. I had this primal urge to do what was needed to protect him and keep him safe. I felt like confessing what I saw happen to the gift shop manager would remove any chance of bringing him home. The way our adoption agency worked, the birth mother has the ultimate choice on which family she places her child with. If I were to bring attention to her crime, there would be

A MULTITUDE OF EMOTIONS

no way that she would still choose us. The attachment I had to Jackson was real, and I couldn't lose him.

We waited outside the doors of the hospital, neither of us saying a word. All of a sudden a hospital security guard walked toward us and asked us to step back inside. I could barely breathe. This was the most scary and unnerving situation of my life. He walked us over to the information counter and asked Anna to empty her backpack.

I could not believe what I saw, at least ten different wallets: some new, some old, and some full of random papers and credit cards. At the bottom of her bag was the wallet she had stolen from the gift shop, the tag still on. The security guard picked it up, and she said quickly, "I bought that at Justin's Boots, I have the receipt at home, I can prove it to you." He then asked her for her name and phone number. She spat out a random array of numbers, looked back at me, and winked.

The officer then looked at me and asked for my information. This stressed me and made me shake with fear and frustration because you are not supposed to exchange personal information with birth parents at this step in the adoption process. I begrudgingly answered him.

The security guard asked sternly, "What are you doing here?"

I quickly and quietly answered, "I am accompanying Anna to her appointments today, and we are waiting for a ride to pick her up."

127

I started to cry, and one of the gift shop workers brought me a box of tissues. By this time there was a crowd gathered around us; we were a full spectacle. The officer asked Anna what she was doing there, and with one hand on her bulging belly and one finger pointed at me, she said, "I was at my baby's doctor appointments. Look at this lady right here, she can't even have babies because she has cancer! And I am giving her this baby so she can have one!"

I was left breathless—that stomp on my cancer shadow knocked the air out of me. I felt the world spin around me. Anna carried on about the wallet, unrelenting that she had bought it elsewhere. I was learning quickly about a life I did not know, recognizing how green to the world I was. A million thoughts crossed my mind, the most prevalent being gratitude for my parents' love.

I must have disassociated for a moment because it seemed like I blinked and the gift shop worker was walking back to her store with the wallet in hand, Anna was placing her collection of goods in her bag, and the crowd had dispersed. I saw one of the other social workers from the adoption agency, Mercy, walk through the door toward us, her face furrowed with confusion. Mercy quickly asked us what was happening as the security guard was walking away. I started to speak, and Anna spoke over me, sharing a diluted version of the truth. As we made our way to the hospital's exit, Anna walked too close to me, and whispered in my ear, "I don't like it when people don't trust me."

I drove home in a fugue, surprised I made it to my front door. Our house was unusually full, my in-laws, Alma and Richard, were there, as was a college friend, Robbie. I had to snap into normal life more quickly than my body was ready; we loaded Louis into his car seat and drove downtown to celebrate Alma's birthday at A Dopo Pizza. I had to compartmentalize my thoughts and be in the present moment. We all sat down to order and eat. My phone rang and it was Jane, the social worker. I stepped outside to answer the call.

Mercy had taken Anna to Walmart to pick up a few necessities. Part of the adoption agency's mission is to care for birth mothers, providing whatever they need. As they were leaving the store, a manager came running after them. Somehow they knew that Anna had stolen items from the store. This was not her first time stealing from this store, so they called the police. Jane was calling to let me know that Anna was in jail, and that was a good thing. While in jail, she would only be given the exact medications that her doctors had prescribed for her.

At this moment everything made sense. I was suddenly thrust into the depths of the opioid crisis. Jane told me not to worry, that Jackson was in the safest place he could be at the moment. I hung up the phone and doubled over, letting out a primal scream. Tears streamed out of my eyes faster than my body could keep up with them. I cried, releasing a multitude of emotions.

I had an unearthly connection to Jackson. I knew that he was my son, and I wanted to protect him and keep him safe. I could not believe that he was in jail and that it was the safest place for him to be. The fact that Anna stole from the hospital gift shop and then went right to Walmart and stole again—I could not comprehend it. I stood there, in front of that restaurant, crying, scared, and frustrated. The only witnesses to this were the entirety of the band Judah and the Lion, as they were playing a show nearby later that night and were waiting outside the restaurant.

I finally caught my breath and returned inside to let Joseph know about the call. Repeating the information Jane gave me made it sound even more unbelievable. This could not be reality. But it was: our baby was in jail, and we were told to think positively about this, he was safe. With all of this completely out of my control, I had to return to hope, to believe that everything was somehow going to be okay.

22

THE BIRTH OF JACK

For the next few days, I kept my phone in my hand, waiting for a call for information. Being able to take care of Louis at this time was a welcome distraction for my heart. He was two and a half and the sweetest toddler; he was balm for my spirit. Eventually, Anna was released from jail, and Jane picked her up. The agency continued to help Anna and Dustin with anything they needed. Jane passed along a handwritten apology letter from Anna. She shared things about her life that helped me have compassion for her, as understanding will usually lead you to it.

I attended another OB appointment with Anna, Jane, and my mother-in-law, Alma. I needed a person to ground me, to help keep my mind safe during what would assuredly be a difficult experience. I hadn't seen Anna since our previous gift shop escapade, and I was nervous to do so. My inner desire to see Jackson's sonogram and hear his heartbeat was stronger than any other feeling or thought I was having.

I was calmed by seeing his outline on that small screen and hearing the pitter-patter of his heart. Alma and I were in the room when her OB saw her this time, and Anna was showing off bruises from having fallen onto furniture while having a seizure. It seemed like every second I was in the presence of Anna, I was learning something unexpected about her. It was hard for me to separate the feelings of shock and of fear for the baby inside her body, as well as the curiosity I had about her, wondering what her childhood was like and how a person finds themselves in her exact place in life.

As we left the room, I watched Anna beeline for a nurses' station, asking for diapers and formula. The nurse responded quickly that she was given these items at one of her previous visits, and they would not be giving them to her again. Anna had a very hard time accepting this truth, to say the least. As we walked out of the hospital, Anna told all of us she was just trying to get the diapers and formula for Jackson and that he deserved to have them. Alma and I said a quick good-bye and walked quietly to our car. As we left the parking garage, I saw Anna sitting on a picnic table in a hospital courtyard smoking a cigarette. I said a silent prayer over Jackson as a tear rolled down my cheek.

I felt with all my heart that Jackson was my child; it is difficult to explain the maternal instincts that were present in my body at that time. Adoption is mysterious in this way; trying to explain our connection is like trying to explain why the sun shines.

As parents, our number one job is to keep our children safe, but at this time, Jackson's safety was completely out of my control, out of my reach. The only thing I could do was pray to God for protection over his body, just as we prayed for Louis while he endured chemotherapy.

A few days later we received the call that Anna was going into labor, and it was time to head into the hospital. We met Dustin and Jane in a waiting area, and I was escorted to their delivery room. Anna was resting when I came into the room. I sat by her side until she opened her eyes. She was happy to see me, we made small talk, and she asked, "Are you ready to see your boy?"

Several hours passed of nurses coming in to check on Anna, and labor slowly progressed. Then early in the morning of May 7, 2018, with Dustin holding one hand, and me holding the other, Anna pushed Jackson out and into the world. In that moment she was my hero. I was so thankful that she chose us to parent Jackson and proud of her for birthing him. This was the only delivery I had ever witnessed other than my own. The miracle of childbirth is a display of the human body performing at its best. I couldn't believe I was able to be, to quote Lin-Manuel Miranda, "in the room where it happened."

A nurse took Jackson over to the warming table to get him cleaned up, and lucky for me, I just walked over to it. I wasn't lying in a hospital bed, exhausted from childbirth; I was full of energy, ready to hold and love him. I felt such peace that he was there, on the table screaming. His face looked scrunched up and mad, his hair was sticking straight up, and he reminded me of Anger from the movie *Inside Out*. They wrapped him up and handed him to Anna. She snuggled him, whispering words into his ear, for only him to hear.

The room was full of people, as it always is right after childbirth. I was an extra body in the way and found myself pushed to the perimeter of the room, becoming a wallflower. I wanted to hold him so bad, to have skin-to-skin time, and tell him how much he was loved. But no one brought him to me; at that moment in time I was nothing.

Eventually, the room emptied, and it was just me and Anna left. I think she forgot about me, as I remained in the corner, but once she noticed me, I told her thank you and that I would go talk to Joseph and let him know Jackson was here. I found him quickly and went in for a long hug, out of both celebration and concern. We had to hold many emotions at once and be prepared for anything to happen.

We went to the nursery window and could see the nurses weighing Jackson and checking him over. A smiling social worker showed us to our room. As the adoptive parents, we were given a postpartum room to receive the baby when it was our turn to have him. The nurses were in charge of delivering him in between our room and his birth parent's room.

Later that evening we heard a knock on the door, and a nurse pushed his hospital bassinet through. This would be the first time we ever held him, calming my frantic heart. His hair was strawberry blond, and his blue eyes wandered around the room. He was very aware and seemed to be looking for our faces. We had lots of skin-to-skin time and told him how much we loved him. The nurse returned and said that his birth parents wanted to keep him in their room over-night. We kissed him good-bye and went home. We were exhausted from being awake for so long, but also fearful that Anna and Dustin would change their minds about us.

Because of their history, Anna and Dustin could not take Jackson home from the hospital, but they still had the right to choose whom he went home with, and we did not want to ruffle any feathers. We enjoyed sleeping in our own bed that night and rushed back to the hospital in the morning, only to find out that Jackson had spent the night in the nursery, which broke our hearts. We had a friend meet us there to take newborn pictures of Jackson, and as we started taking pictures, the tremors started.

23

A ROOM FOR CRYING

We quickly learned that Jackson was withdrawing from the various substances that he had been exposed to in utero. The medical diagnosis for this is neonatal abstinence syndrome, NAS for short. I knew nothing about this but learned quickly, it is the unfortunate outcome for the precious babies impacted by the opioid crisis.

After the photos were finished, a nurse came to take Jackson back to Anna's room, as she had requested time with him. He was starting to struggle, and it was so hard to let him go. About ten minutes passed, and I realized his pacifier was still in our room. I picked it up and went to deliver it to him. I found Anna's room and knocked on the door. I heard her say, "Come in," so I opened the door. Jackson was in his little bed, alone, right by the door. Anna was across the room staring out the window. I said, "Excuse me, Anna," and she turned around slowly, "Oh, sorry I didn't hear you. I was just praying." I gave Jackson his pacifier and slowly walked out of the room.

Confusion and frustration overtook my mind. I decided on that short walk back to our room that I needed a shift in Jackson's name, to give my heart some space from Anna. I told Joseph that I needed us to start using the name Jack. I needed him to hear my voice over everything else and for him to know it was me. From that moment on, we called him Jack.

A nurse brought Jack back to us a little bit later, and as we held him, his tremors had worsened, and he began to cry out in a high-pitched sound, a little kitty cat begging for relief. A social worker came in and let us know the plan.

"He is beginning to withdraw and needs to go to the NICU at Children's Hospital. Gather your things, and you can meet Jack in his new room across the street."

They had a special underground tunnel to transport babies from the hospital where he was born to the NICU at Children's. We rushed over as fast as we could, signed in, and made our way to Jack.

A doctor came into the room and gave us a rundown of what was happening. The doctors used a system to score the babies, to see how much medication they needed, called the Finnegan Scoring System. They would rate the baby's metabolic, respiratory, gastrointestinal, and central nervous systems. They then compiled the numbers to move forward with treatment. After a day of treatment, they would reassess symptoms and move the dosage up or down to help the baby detox with as little pain as possible. The goal is to give a NAS baby a controlled version of one of the substances they were exposed to, taper it off as the days go on, and the baby becomes accustomed to life.

My mind was going a million miles a minute. All of these words for different types of opioids were being tossed around, and me standing there without any prior knowledge of what an opioid even was. Did I use an opioid when I had my wisdom teeth removed in high school? I couldn't even remember.

I was learning every second that this was a world that I knew nothing of, but it was all Jack knew. They tested his systems, gave him his Finnegan score, and administered his first dose of medication, morphine sulfate. Everything was happening quickly, nurses here and there. But once it was given, the room slowed down, and the social worker stayed behind to help answer our questions.

Jack would need a room for crying. He needed to be able to wail without disrupting any other babies. His crying was inevitable; the medication administered only took the edge off. We learned that he had lived his entire life in utero accustomed to a cocktail of medications, so that was the only way his body knew how to exist.

As the various drugs' half lives came to fruition, he began to writhe in pain, withdrawing as an adult would. From a test of the blood in his umbilical cord, the doctors knew of seven products present in his system. It was a guessing game as to what would be needed to alleviate his pain, and as the days carried on, my hate for opioids grew.

This innocent two-day-old baby was bearing the weight of an epidemic. Jack was the collateral damage of the opioid crisis. Anna said that she did not know she was pregnant until late in her pregnancy. She disclosed this to her pain-management doctors, and they told her she had to continue whatever she was using because if she stopped, the baby would detox in utero and die.

24

No External Stimuli

﹏✦﹏

We began our second stint of NICU parenting, remembering our six days with Louis back in the NICU in North Carolina. I told myself over and over, "there is no easy way for us to bring home a baby." We were strangely prepared for this. The nurses taught us how to care for Jack. Babies with NAS have various needs; you have to try things and see how they respond. Most like to be swaddled tight, with little external stimulation, and held as much as possible. When it was time to give Jack a bottle, we would pick him up, swaddle him tight, and, without any noise, give him his bottle. He could not stand any stimulation, not even a smell; we had to wear scentless deodorant and lotion.

At the start of his detox, he did not want to be held. I imagined his skin hurt while we were holding him. It was mottled, with little webs of purple spread under the top layer of his skin, covering his whole body. When a wave of pain went through him, his face would scrunch up in agony, and sometimes instead of crying out, there was just a silent yelp.

His tremors continued, and the morphine helped, but it did not take away any symptoms completely. This was the same type of morphine that is used in end-of-life care; the irony of him beginning his life with it is not lost on me. A few other symptoms he experienced were excessive sneezing, yawning, and tight muscle tone. His arms and legs felt almost like they were being flexed, not the normal softness of a baby but a hard and tense surface. He constantly needed a paci, and it seemed as though the sucking helped relieve some pain.

Joseph and I got into a rhythm: I would stay at the NICU all day with Jack, and he would go to work. My parents were at our house with Louis, keeping him in his daily routine. Joseph would leave work, head straight to the hospital, and we would switch out. I would rush home to Louis, to spend time with him, and Joseph took the night shift with Jack, getting up every three hours as he needed bottles and to be rocked to sleep. I would wake up in the morning and drive straight to the hospital, Joseph would leave for work, and we would do it all over again.

After a week and a half of the detox process using morphine, something was still amiss. We thought he was improving, but he still exhibited some concerning symptoms. The doctors decided the best course of action was to give him clonidine, used as a sedative, so his body could detox another type of drug without as much pain. This was a heartbreaking time because he could barely be awake for his bottles. The sadness I felt for him was balanced by peace, knowing that he was avoiding some pain.

Jack spent twelve days in the NICU. Anna and Dustin came to visit him one day; they brought him two little race cars that Dustin had painted just for him. During our NICU stay, they also went to the courthouse and signed away their parental rights, allowing us to be able eventually to adopt Jack. They had three full days after signing to change their mind. This was a very stressful time, as we were deep in the NICU life of caring for Jack, all while wondering what was happening in the legal world of our adoption. Some adoptive parents choose not to be involved with a baby until the birth parents' rights are fully terminated, but we could not imagine Jack going through his NICU stay without a support system.

When we were finally able to bring him home, both sets of grandparents and Louis were there waiting to see him. Louis asked, "Can I take him to the basement to play on a little trampoline?" It was a sweet moment to have our whole family under one roof for the first time. This was a big change for all of us, especially Jack. He had only known the quiet that was his room in the

NICU, and we quickly figured out we needed to replicate that for him to be able to take his bottles.

He truly needed no external stimuli to be able to focus on eating, and with Louis being just under three years old, that was difficult. We had to get creative. We put a rocking chair in a bedroom, closed the curtains, turned on a sound machine, swaddled him tight in a blanket, and gave Louis an iPad so he would be occupied. This was a high-stakes operation, because Jack needed to get his calories in, and the stars had to align in our home for that to be able to happen, and it was every few hours. The Lord made a way, and Louis loved getting to watch KidsTube and Jack began to gain weight. My mother-in-law, Alma, gave us the Baby Brezza, which was like a Keurig coffee maker but for baby formula, which helps in making bottles quickly.

When Louis was a baby, I fought to be able to nurse him. I pushed my body to make milk for him because I wasn't going to let cancer take that opportunity from him. Louis stopped nursing on his own, at around twenty months of age.

I knew that I would not be able to nurse Jack; there are ways to trick your body into lactating for bringing home a baby via adoption, but I was fearful to put my body through that. I was deeply afraid that my body would think I was pregnant and I would relapse, my leukemia rushing back into my life. This may have been a distorted way to think, but I needed to protect my body and my family from the possibility.

The way God provided milk for Jack is one of the many miracles I've witnessed in my life. In preparation for bringing Jack home, I reached out to friends who had recently had babies and asked for donor milk. And they delivered! These women were so giving of their time and energy for my baby. I started locally, and friends in the Knoxville area would deliver milk to my doorstep, even loading it into my freezer for me. I would make bottles for Jack with one-quarter of the contents being donor milk and three-quarters of the contents being formula. I wanted to make the donor milk last as long as possible. When our supply ran low, I would reach out to various friends. I remember Amber bringing me two bags she had pumped just to get me through a few more days. They say breast milk is liquid gold, and I treated it as such.

I would post on social media about how thankful we were for these gifts of milk, and it would bring this issue to the attention of distant friends. They wanted to be involved too. Malorie, a highschool classmate, knew of a coworker who wanted to donate a freezer full of pumped milk to a family with an adopted baby. She loaded the milk in her car in Greenville, North Carolina, drove it to our mutual hometown, to meet my parents in a Kmart parking lot, who then drove it to me. Another friend, Ashley, had a similar situation. She brought milk from her friend to my little brother, Erick. He put it in a friend's deep freezer and delivered it to Anna K, who then brought it to my front door as she headed home for the holidays. I even had two friends who had donated milk to Louis also donate to Jack.

I kept count of how many ladies donated to Jack—it was fourteen! Because of their unwavering support and offering, Jack had donor milk in every single bottle he drank for the first fourteen months of his life. I realize this is a hot-button issue in the mom community, and many say, "Fed is best." And I agree, you have to feed your baby in a way that is beneficial to you and your baby. But for me, I needed to give Jack the same opportunity as Louis to receive the antibodies and goodness that come from breast milk. I prayed for this and God delivered. There should be a medical study on Jack's immune system: he never gets sick, and if he does, he moves through it quickly. I believe the milk from different women made his body super immune. He has only had five fevers in his life, has no allergies or skin problems, and as he likes to comment, his hair is "bright and shiny."

In December of 2018, we drove to the courthouse in Knoxville and met with a judge. We agreed to love Jack just as we love Louis, promising to take care of him for our whole lives. Our family and friends gathered around us as we celebrated Jack officially becoming a member of our family. We made his name official, adding Collins to be his middle name. This was Luci's last name, and we wanted to honor her legacy. This day was sweet, but we had already felt all of those things.

From the moment I heard of his existence, I had what could only be described as a supernatural connection to Jack. By some miracle and force greater than myself, I knew in my heart I was going to love and care for him forever.

25

ᴄFULL ᴄGIRCLE
ᴄMOMENT

We were relieved when we made it through the newborn stage with Jack! Louis was in preschool at the time, so he had social interaction with peers, and I had one-on-one time with Jack. Because of his NAS, we had access to various forms of early intervention. Different therapists would come to our home and teach me how to take care of him in the best way possible, using various massages and arm and leg movements to help with his tight muscle tone. They taught me tricks to get him to eat, allowing him to rest to regain strength.

We also had access to the Grow With Me clinic at our Children's Hospital, one of the only groups in the country researching NAS children. When we had our visits there, Jack was evaluated by every type of therapist you can think of; their goal was to give early intervention for any issue that may arise. This clinic had only been open for three years before Jack was born, so their research on NAS babies was only three years older than he was at the time. We were in essence growing alongside the clinic and their research.

When Jack was about fifteen months old, we received a very strange call. Jane, the social worker from our adoption agency, called to let us know Anna was very sick. She asked if I would like to visit her, and I did. I laid aside my many conflicted feelings and visited her in the hospital. We made small talk, and Anna let me know what was happening.

"I have cancer. It's spreading through me like wildfire." Anna's words took the breath out of my lungs.

"Is there anything I can bring you, anything to make you more comfortable?" I asked in earnest. Her only request was a Bible that she could understand.

A few days later I returned with a copy of *The Jesus Storybook Bible* by Sally Lloyd-Jones. "Can you read me a story? One about Jesus?"

What a special, unexpected moment of sharing Jesus with her.

It's a memory I hold dear in my heart. A moment of peace in the midst of tragedy.

"Is there was anything you want me to tell Jack, anything you want him to know?"

"Please be sure to sing to him 'Simple Man' by Lynyrd Skynyrd. That is what I want for him."

We said our good-byes, I said a quick prayer, and left. A few days later I received a call that she had passed away.

The full circle moment, of me surviving cancer and Anna dying from cancer, was almost too much for me to bear. At first I felt sadness, because any death is a loss, a future gone. Then there was survivor guilt, more reasons to wonder why I continued to live when it seemed as though everyone else who had cancer died. But the place I landed on was mercy. Mercy has a way of doing that, leading and landing us where we least expect sometimes.

This mercy was a gift for our Jack, that we could tell him about how Anna passed away, at the hands of cancer, a subject our family understood all too well. Cancer seems, after all, to be an acceptable way to die. Never frowned upon by society, never leading others to investigate or judge life choices. When a person has cancer, every other aspect of them falls away; they suddenly have a singularity that no one can see around, a concept I am awfully familiar with. In Anna's death, there was a new life opportunity, a control-alt-delete in erasing her past and replacing it with social acceptance. Like mercy, sometimes cancer has a way of leading and landing us where we least expect as well.

I still carried conflicted feelings toward Anna. I was thankful that she chose us to be Jack's parents. But at the same time I struggled not to stay stuck in the quicksand of my mind. After all, Jack was the collateral damage of not only Anna's personal choices but the opioid crisis at large, and I needed someone or something to blame. He did nothing to deserve this entrance into life.

I blamed Anna. I judged her. I put myself on a pedestal above her.

I could never hurt a baby. I would always keep my children safe.

However, while processing her death, I had a stark realization: she and I were more similar than I had realized.

Anna and I were both fighting diseases. In our pregnancies, me with Louis and her with Jack, we were both fighting our own personal nightmares. We both exposed our babies to toxins and trauma in the name of survival.

I could have made a different choice; I could have forgone chemotherapy to protect Louis from unknown harms. My oncologists told me it would have been a death sentence for me, but Louis would have survived. I live with this unsettled fear buried deep inside me, wondering if he will develop some random ailment from his chemo exposure. He did not deserve any harm, but he needed his mother. My survival outweighed any possible infringement to him; when my mind takes me to these thoughts, I feel like I have been punched in the gut, the air removed from my lungs.

Anna and I had parallel yet unique experiences in our respective battles. Louis and Jack shared a kind of kindred pregnancy, both pushing science and medicine to the extreme. Both gestational situations left doctors with raised eyebrows and slumped shoulders that accompanied the unknown.

The human condition is "knotty," and I thank Beth Moore for that word. Life has twists and turns, and none of us crawl through it unscathed. One minor injury, one prescription, could lead anyone to a lifetime of addiction. I learned that many of the things Anna was addicted to she sadly had prescriptions for. The substances that affected Jack were created to prevent a person who struggles with addiction from overdosing. They are as lifesaving as chemotherapy.

Addiction is complicated, and the greed of the pharmaceutical companies that produce these highly addictive opioids speaks for itself. From what I have observed, there is an endless system upheld by bureaucracy and deep pockets causing this epidemic to continue to incur undue injury and death upon so many.

I will never understand how Anna's situation came to be. I will never fully know all there is to know about her childhood dreams and young adult life. This information is not for me to know. For some reason, we were brought into each other's lives, and I was gifted with the beautiful responsibility of raising our boys. With the love and safety given to me by my parents, coupled hugely with my faith, I can be the mother I need to be for our boys. I will walk with them through this life for as many miles as my feet will take me.

26

ONE MINUTE AT A TIME

No doctor or nurse could tell me exactly how life was going to pan out for Jack; there is no way to know how NAS will affect his future. It affects every child differently, and the research is too young to give any solid information. So, we did what we had to do every day to love and care for him. Louis became the best big brother, watching over Jack and bringing him toys and blankets. I was thrilled to have two boys to care for and a loving husband; our family was complete.

Jane, from our adoption agency, asked if we wanted to meet one of Jack's siblings and his mom. We jumped at this opportunity and had Nicholas and Carrie over to our house as soon as possible. This was a divine introduction, watching two brothers, just a year apart, meet and interact. This began a friendship between our families that is one of my favorite gifts. As Louis loves to explain the situation to friends, "Nicholas is Jack's brother, but he isn't my brother. I do love him like a brother, so it's kind of like he is my brother."

Carrie and I are raising full brothers, only living twenty minutes apart. It is such a blessing to be able to ask her about medical and behavior-related issues. It's like having an extra parent in our family. Nicholas and Jack are magnets. When they spend time together, they wrestle and play with the same level of fervor and energy. At this time, Jack is a bit confused about Nicholas being his brother, as biological and adoptive siblings are not easy subjects to understand for a child, but I pray that one day they will understand how special their relationship is.

We were just cruising right along in life, until March 2020 hit. The COVID-19 virus caused the world to shut down, begging us to stay safe at home. Just as a reminder, in 2015 I spent seven months in and out of the hospital in almost complete isolation, at times not even being allowed to touch another human. I spent the first year of Louis's life at home, regaining my strength slowly and tending to his growing body. In 2018 we stayed home for most of the year because external stimuli bothered Jack to the point that if he became overstimulated, he could not eat or sleep for the next several hours. By the time the pandemic came and went, I had spent almost all of my postgraduate life in some form of isolation.

I leaned into the stay-at-home orders and decided to make the most of it. I figured out how to schedule our day, with playtime, screen time, and nap time. Joseph was never able to work from home, so I counted down the minutes until his return home each day, eager for a bit of relief.

This time was taxing and difficult for us, as it was for everyone. Those of you who were taking care of babies or the elderly know how this time weighed on our hearts. I felt like I was running a toddler day camp. Many days, I would tackle things an hour at a time, and on the hardest days, I took things one minute at a time.

One way we made it through that season was by dancing in the kitchen. I thought about my abuelita and how she moved through her home. Always young at heart, her spirit seemed to be floating in another plane of existence. I can imagine her hips swaying as she worked in the kitchen, adding vegetables to a big stock pot for soup. I embodied her spirit for my boys. I added fun playlists of music to our Alexa to keep our spirits high.

I would put on John Mayer or The Avett Brothers, and we would have a kitchen dance party, Jack in his footie jammies and Louis with his big smile. We would sing and dance, infusing joy into our otherwise mundane days.

When Kristen Bell convinced Disney to release *Frozen 2* on Disney+, our lives were saved. We watched that movie twice a day. I would make myself a dalgona coffee and snuggle up on the couch with the boys.

That movie was like a magic healing balm, guiding us through our long and lonely days. Looking back, I am thankful for extra time with my boys at home, with nowhere to go and nothing to do. However, I hope we never have to go through another global pandemic in our lifetime.

Toward the end of the pandemic, Jack received outpatient occupational therapy to help with fine motor skills. He did not love this experience, as he only wanted to participate in activities that used gross motor skills. We were learning quickly that there was something unique about his brain. Once he was able to walk, he never fell. He could run down a hill, with rocks and roots sticking up, and never fall. I eventually stopped using phrases like "be careful" and "watch out" because it didn't matter. He never got hurt. He never got sick, and he was a wonderful sleeper.

He was cute as a button, but he had trouble keeping his body regulated and struggled with impulse control. If someone was playing with blocks, he would knock them down. When it came time to eat a meal, he could hardly sit to eat. We used toys to keep him occupied at the table, because he would play as we put food in his mouth. He desperately needed to spend as much time outside as possible; it seemed like the more time he had outside, the better he was able to regulate his body and emotions while he was inside.

There were times when he felt out of control, especially after a nap. He would cry and scream for an hour, and the only thing that seemed to help was for me to hold him chest to chest and walk around the house. Over and over I would circle the inside perimeter of our house, trying to soothe him. If I got tired and stopped walking, he would cry more, so I had to keep walking.

I researched the different sensory systems of the body and learned how to help him calm them down. I had no previous knowledge of the vestibular or proprioception systems, but I had to learn. I would spin him in circles, put him in a swing, or have him jump up and down to help bring his mind back to a safe space.

We had to live our life in a way where either Joseph or I could escape any public situation with Jack at any moment. He seemed to be easily overstimulated in large groups of people, so sitting down to eat a meal at a restaurant was nearly impossible.

When he was the ages two through four, he hardly went anywhere; he was a COVID toddler. Is it possible that we missed a window of opportunity to slowly teach him how to behave in a restaurant? He didn't get to eat inside a restaurant until he was over four years old, and he didn't understand why he couldn't get up from our table and run around, which is understandable.

We loved our family, but some things felt more difficult than expected. Long car rides would make Jack scream. The hardest thing was his inability to remain in control over his body, as if he needed to ram into another person in order to ground himself. We started going to a child psychologist to learn how to help him. I had tried everything under the sun, but I was not enough. I was grappling with the trauma from his in-utero experience, trying to make sense of it all.

One day as I was discussing this with the nurse practitioner at the Grow With Me clinic, one of the world's experts in NAS, she said something that changed my heart and gave me peace.

"I see many babies come in and out of this clinic, and I can see the progress he is making. Your love has rewired his brain." This verbal acknowledgment poured water into my soul; it gave me strength to continue to dig deep and care for Jack to the absolute best of my ability.

Many of you are aware of the term *crosscultural adoption*. In most cases in the United States, this refers to a white couple adopting a black child. There is much to say about this and much research on how to do this well. There is a lot to learn about making sure a child has appropriate role models, is introduced to music and television where they see themselves on screen, and has access to and knowledge of appropriate hair care. No one talks about a half-Latina adopting a fully Caucasian baby. I have had to walk this road alone. I have had to endure comments from strangers over and over again that make me want to fall into a sink-hole. The summer sun darkens my skin and lightens his hair, widening the divide between our respective gene pools.

Jack is old enough now that I fear these comments will fill his brain with undue doubt. If I am out in the world with just the boys, people comment on how much Louis and I look alike. This is true: we are twins, and he is my mini me. They first comment on our likeness, and then they comment on Jack's difference.

They will say something to the effect of, "Wow, I would think the little blond would look more like you." To which I only muster, "Yup." There is no easy way to handle this at the moment; I want to end the conversation as quickly as possible.

All the available options stink, proof that real-world and digital interactions vary wildly. On the internet, I could ignore or delete any uncomfortable comments. In real life, in the presence of my children, my options are limited. I will never, ever say back, "Well, you are astute in your observance. The blond-haired blue-eyed boy would be genetically impossible for me to procreate." Or, "He is adopted, and that is why he looks so different from me." Or, "No, I am not the Latina nanny for a nuclear scientist family."

When the four of us are out together, it's a different experience. People always comment on how cute our family is; one son looks just like the mom, and one son looks just like the dad. I recently learned that a new friend assumed we were a blended family. Joseph and Jack share many traits. And I am thankful for that. I know this will add to Jack's sense of belonging as he grows. The more Joseph is in the sun, his hair turns shades of blond to match Jack's, and they have the same build, tall and lean. Jack will put on a three-button henley shirt and comment on how much he looks like Daddy. He loves his resemblance to Joseph, and we lean into that when we can. I am thankful we have these experiences as a family of four in public, to balance the hard times when it's just me and the boys. Adoption is its own miracle. I cannot explain it. The gift of it is beautiful but always accompanied by pain. There is no adoption story without loss. There are grief and unanswered questions. Lots of "who lived in which belly" conversations in our home. We talk about it openly and let our boys lead the way. With patience, we listen and reassure.

In writing this memoir, I had doubts about what to share, as this is such a sensitive and difficult subject. However, this is our true story. This is how our sunshine Jack came into our lives. This is one example of how an adoption happened and how our lives were forever changed by Anna and Dustin choosing us to be Jack's forever family.

27

REPEAT THE SOUNDING JOY

~⌒~

I never worked outside our home. I have never been paid monetarily for anything since having cancer and children. I was encouraged to go to college and get a degree. Then I would be able to get a job in a desirable career field. I paid my dues and worked hard to receive scholarships. My parents sacrificed to cover the rest of my education and allowed me to graduate debt-free. I was the first person in my family to graduate from college, and I wore that badge proudly. I needed to use this newly acquired skill set, which was seven years in the making, to prove all the sacrifice that was made for me had been worth it. I was full of enthusiasm to get into a school system and change the lives of students.

I had dreams of a life that was more than "home-making," which was what the women in the generations before me did. That was admirable work, but I had the degrees, baby. I was going to do it all. Work-life balance never occurred to me back in college. However, I fall into a category with many of my peers where we quickly realized in this modern economy, we could not have it all.

Having children and both parents working felt impossible. I, along with many other college-degree-holding moms, deferred our dreams of careers and working outside the home. The numbers were too skewed—the low pay that most of us would receive compared to the higher pay of our male counter-parts—would barely cover the cost of child care. Add in all the days kiddos end up being home from day care or school because of illness, I would be working part-time. It was a frustrating racket. We were told to go to college, then get a substantial career *and* start a family, but there were no systems in place to support all of it.

Two resources have been created to aid families in navigating work-life-family balance. CARRY Media was founded by Paula Faris, whose mission is to champion and advocate for working moms through storytelling. In addition, a new system created by Eve Rodsky is aiming to teach couples to divide household labor. You can find Rodsky's information in book and documentary form by the name of *Fair Play*. Both of these resources aim to aid families in learning how to exist in our modern world in a way where everyone feels appreciated and successful.

Before these wonderful ladies put their ideas out in the world for me to consume, I had to make the most of what I could, with what I had. I took all the knowledge I had gained in college, from my master's degree in school counseling, and in life overall to care for my boys. I gave them all that I had to give and more. I went to bed exhausted every night but prayed daily for the strength to tend to and love my children. I made them my whole life, out of necessity but also discombobulation.

Taking care of my babies made sense to me; it was easier to be a stay-at-home mom with no other responsibilities. I was not beholden to anyone for anything. I did not have the slightest clue how to enter society as a mother, wife, and person. It all felt like too much.

No one tells you how to be an adult. When we were learning algebra and the layers of the earth's core, we should have been learning how to sign up for health insurance and get our taxes turned in on time. We should have been taught what it takes to keep a home peaceful and stocked with food, how to stop kids' snack-bar wrappers from filling the floorboard of your vehicle. How often to call your grandma to check in, how to keep up with yearly physicals and dental appointments, and when to change your air filters. How to juggle friendships, marital relationships, self-care, ironing dress shirts, field trip permission forms, Christmas presents for teachers, asking your coworker about their aunt who is in hospice. It is a lot. To quote Kate Bowler, "There is no cure for being human."

At the beginning of motherhood, my focus was tiny, singular. It was just me and Louis, then Joseph when he got home from work. Next, we added in Jack, and we had a little quartet of love and needs. I tended to these relationships like a garden with all of my mind, heart, and soul. Audrey Hepburn once said, "To plant a garden is to believe in tomorrow," and I think the same is true for young motherhood.

You give your children love and a profound sense of belonging with hopes that those roots will remain strong throughout their lives. You hope and pray that the belonging they felt in childhood will bloom and grow throughout their lives, giving them a deep anchor of love to hold on to in life's hardest moments.

I desire to provide my children with a safe place to land when the outside world becomes too much. I think of our old friend from Boiling Springs, DT, when I softly tell them, "I love you no matter what." I want my boys to know that there is nothing that can keep me from loving them. I need to prove what the word *unconditional* means.

I know the love of my mother is the one defining factor that allowed me to survive the fastballs life threw my way. Her unconditional love through my childhood and young adulthood gave me inner strength; I knew I had a deep well of support to draw from at any moment. The grit and resolve I gained from external childhood difficulties (mainly middle school boys) balanced with the support I always knew to be present was the perfect combination to guide me, to give me courage. I can take what I need from my past and "repeat the sounding joy" to my children.

PART 4

TODAY

28

WHY I SURVIVED

ventually, Louis went to kindergarten and Jack started preschool, and my world changed. I could care for myself in a way that I could not in the weeds of young motherhood. I was able to expand my relational radius and cultivate my growing friendships. I returned to the gym and found myself working out for the right reasons. COVID-19 restrictions eased, and I was able to volunteer in Louis's classroom. I slowly learned how to broaden my life and be open to possibilities outside my home.

I also found myself able to conceptualize the last eight years. I had time to reevaluate and rediscover myself. I was able to consider my eventful life and unearth where I landed. Until this point I had lived my whole adult life in a form of survival mode—moving from one traumatic experience to the next.

I had to come to terms with being a survivor. I needed to. I grappled with the concept that I was alive and so many others who battled cancer, specifically AML, did not survive. I would question and ponder. I would cry any time I learned of another human with this diagnosis; I felt that it was a new death sentence, but I was the only one who knew what was coming.

People came to me for hope. Acquaintances would reach out to me and say, "My cousin's husband was just diagnosed with cancer. Could I pass along your contact information?"

I always say yes. "Yes, pass on my name and number." Yes, tell them my story of hope.

Hope is a necessary component of survivorship, but sometimes nothing is enough.

And the more people who contacted me, the list of lost loved ones grew. As did my survivor's guilt.

Recently I had a realization, a truth pushed into the light. This new but obvious understanding came to me while washing dishes, as most good thoughts do. I saw my why in the faces of my boys, Louis and Jack.

Louis with his tender heart and Jack with his magnificent mind.

I knew why I survived. It was for them.

I know there is no one else on Earth to mother them. I had to survive to love and advocate for them. I have the skills required to keep them safe. My childhood, college degrees, and ability to maintain hope all contribute to the cause.

Once I leaned into the reason I survived, the survivor's guilt was finally able to subside. It transferred from the forefront of my mind to the tip of my little toe. Never to be gone completely but out of my daily thought process.

If I ask my boys, "What is my job?" They answer in unison, "To keep us safe."

They know this is my goal and the framework through which all family decisions are made. It's more than just seat belts in the car; it's keeping up to date on research with the effects of screen time and food dyes. It's explaining safe touches and tricky people. It's modeling how to ask for help when I am at the end of my rope. It's understanding their deeply unique personalities and being patient through frustrations. I did not know how much patience parenting requires, but that is the main fruit of the Spirit that I pray for every day.

Earlier this year, Joseph was struggling with the stressors of his job and the desire to spend more time with our family. He was feeling pulled in every direction constantly, never feeling like he was able to catch up in any area of his life. He wanted to be the best husband, coworker, son, friend, and father he could be, but you cannot excel at all of these elements at the same time. Joseph is the hardest worker you will ever meet, a person you want on your team because he does not know how to quit.

We would have late-night conversations about things we could do to make our lives more manageable.

One day he said, "I just can't wait to be retired and have all the time in the world to do the things we have always wanted to do." Well, this concept is not one that I can understand, as waiting for retirement is not a privilege I have.

No part of my brain can allow me to think of myself at the age of sixty-seven. Who knows when my final days will be? No healthcare professional can answer that question, for me or anyone else. I have trained my brain to be thankful for today and today only.

How can I have respite in a number so far away? I can't rest in both worlds. I don't ponder death; I don't sit around thinking about cancer returning. I have to live in the great unknown, in the present, without fear of death.

I am not afraid of death in and of itself; what I fear is leaving my boys. I'm not afraid to die; I fear being gone. I tremble at the thought of them having no one to call when they experience their first heartbreak. Who would walk them through it? The number of times I have called my mama just to tell her about my peonies blooming! They deserve to have that opportunity too.

I try my hardest to teach them everything I can about life. They know there are two versions of "I Will Always Love You," and Dolly and Whitney both deserve their adoration. They have seen the original *Teenage Mutant Ninja Turtles* movie. They know the goodness of a peanut butter and honey sandwich. Jack always holds branches out of the way for me while we are hiking, and Louis takes an extra snack bar for a friend at school who likes the type I buy. I take the honing of their emotional intelligence and pop culture references very seriously.

Rather than waiting for retirement, the thing I desired was more time with Joseph now. Yes, I agreed with his sentiment of looking forward to retirement. The idea of a life revolving around slow mornings drinking coffee, puttering around the garden, and reading a book in a hammock sounds wonderful but impossible to attain. I truly feared I would never arrive at that season of life; it seemed out of reach.

We were so busy with life and our children that we did not have the opportunity to spend quality time alone. So we made an epic plan. We decided that Joseph would shift his work life to a new schedule of working four days a week. This would mean he would have to work a little bit longer each day but have Fridays off. He took this idea to his boss, Adam, and he agreed. Without question, Adam said, "Do what you need to do."

Back when I was diagnosed with leukemia, we discovered quickly that we had to move to North Carolina for treatment, not knowing how long we would be there. Joseph went to his boss and explained the situation. Adam told him the same thing then: "Do what you need to do, go to North Carolina with Gaby." I don't think many bosses would be willing to support an employee in this way. I needed Joseph for every second of those seven months; his support was essential to my survival. We are forever grateful for Adam and his wife Heather's love during that difficult time.

So for the last year, Joseph and I have spent Fridays together living like retired people, from nine a.m. to three p.m. while our kids are in school. We are intentional with this time, making sure to spend it together, doing things we love. We play pickleball, drink coffee, eat yummy food, and wander the aisles of Costco. This has been the ultimate gift in our life, knowing that every week we are going to be able to enjoy each other. We love our children, but as anyone with little kids knows, you can lose yourself in your care for them. The foundation of our family rests on the love Joseph and I choose to give each other, and ourselves.

29

WHERE THE MAGIC HAPPENS

*B*eing a cancer survivor came with a few require-ments for me. One being existentialism. What was the meaning of all this? How do I use my experi-ence for good? How can I make the tastiest lemonade out of these lemons? How was I one chromosomal genetic abnormality away from death?

Mary Oliver pondered it best: "Doesn't everything die at last, and too soon? Tell me, what is it you plan to do with your one wild and precious life?"

At first, I thought I should use all my energy to change the world. Maybe I would start fundraising for the Leukemia and Lymphoma Society so they can finally discover a cure to beat all blood cancers. Then I thought our family should become a Safe Families home, a weekend respite for children in foster care. I wanted to volunteer for the American Cancer Society. The idea of rocking sweet babies in the NICU at Children's Hospital crossed my mind.

I wanted to make a difference in the world, to help others going through difficult times similar to our journey. If there were meaning and purpose to all that I had experienced, shouldn't it change the world around me? I thought if I volunteered my life away, there could be some sort of cosmic payback for having survived.

Of course, I had changed, understanding so much more that life is a gift. I don't have to tell you that; you know all the tropes that come with cancer survivorship. Our lives become living "gratitude journals." All of us survivors move through a similar process: almost dying, fighting to live, and then appreciating life in a new way. It is impossible to miss.

But what else? What did I need to do, out there in the world? Could I be happy if all I did was "go home and love my family"? Would that have been a waste of energy and experience? I was searching for a way to unwrap the gift of survivorship and use it in a way that would be authentic to me.

The concept that shifted my course was something my pastor, Lee, said one Sunday at church. He was talking about happiness. He commented on how we all struggle with searching for outside sources of joy. Reaching for our phones or remotes to feel something. He speculated that if a person could not be happy alone in an empty room, then they could not ever be truly happy. That if we are looking for an outward sense of joy or meaning, it is false. True peace and joy are inside us; we just have to slow down long enough to engage with ourselves and God.

This is an inside-out process, one that I need to repeat daily. Removing undue expectations from others and myself. Leaning into ancient truths that our modern life tries to diminish.

I wasn't going to find happiness on a beach in Tahiti. However breathtaking the views are, you can't take them home with you. Reaching the top of Maslow's hierarchy of needs and arriving at self-actualization by volunteering my life away would not complete me. Rocking babies in the NICU wouldn't change my attitude while unloading the dishwasher at home.

I had to learn two hard truths.

There was nothing I could do to "pay back" for my survival.

And there is nothing extraordinary required of me.

Surviving leukemia was a gift. I am blessed.

Helping Jack find the right size soccer cleat, playing Ninja Turtles with him outside. Snuggling and reading Junie B. Jones with Louis at bedtime. These small, everyday actions and displays of patience and love, that is where the magic happens.

As a mother, I am constantly being asked to be and provide entertainment. And the answer I have landed on for myself is the same thing I tell my boys: most of life is boring.

The word *boring* usually has a negative connotation, but I use it in a neutral tone. Boring is neither bad nor exciting. It is cozy. It is comfortable. It is normal. It is a new opportunity to be creative or be created.

After living through cancer, adoption, and COVID-19, settling into a boring routine of life feels good. I feel so strongly about the concept of boring, that I almost titled this book *Boring Is Better*.

I gently guide my little ducklings through their inevitable moments of boredom. I tell them that grabbing a book off the shelf is as good as it gets for this moment between homework and dinner. Children think living in a "mountain-top experience" is the goal. But as adults, we know most of life is a valley, and after all, a valley is where the most beautiful flowers grow.

I try to convey, without breaking their spirits, that there is nothing better out there. This is it. If you can fall in love with your actual life, today, then you have made it. You have arrived.

I tell them, "I can't wait to see what you come up with."

I realize this sentiment is one I can have because of my life's passage. Because of the privileged life I live. Because of the worthiness I feel as being loved unconditionally by my parents and husband. Because of the heat radiating through my fireplace. Because of the food in my refrigerator. Because there is a world in which my health could have easily taken a different turn.

I live in a strange reality, one where the boring is acknowledged and gladly accepted because it is better than death.

Tim McGraw almost had it right in his 2004 hit song entitled "Live Like You Were Dying." He beckons us to shift our perspective on life, an easy ask for a cancer survivor; I can't listen to that song without tears streaming down my face. But it needs a slight modification—sorry, Tim.

I think we should consider: live like you are living. For some of you, that may be climbing the Rocky Mountains or going skydiving. But for most of us, myself included, it means putting down my phone and stepping outside. Closing my eyes and hearing the birds sing. Turning my compost pile or asking a friend to go on a walk.

Alastair Humphreys coined the term *microadventures*, and I think it holds the sentiment of what I need to add to my life, to help me feel the beauty and gravity of my time on Earth. I have learned to seek goodness, and the more I look for it, the more I find it.

Dear reader, I wish I could skip the pains of life for you. I wish my story could take hold of your heart and remove all future obstacles. To convince you to live in the moment, to practice gratitude and mindfulness. But I know even my journey cannot stop life as it comes for you. You will face challenges, health scares, and heartache.

My deepest desire then must be that you will remember to cling to hope in the face of despair. That you will lean into that still, small voice that whispers, "You are loved, you are worthy, you are a child of God."

As a woman, the final requirement of cancer survivorship was coming to terms with this body, face, and head full of hair. If you are forced to get down to the nitty-gritty of life, bare bones and bald head, you will shift your perspective on beauty.

It is inevitable.

There is no other way.

Let's start with hair. It has been a roller coaster of emotions for me, thinking that it did not matter in the moment of losing it, then grappling with the fact that, yes, having hair was something that I appreciated but did not realize until it was gone.

Once my hair grew back in, the chemo curls were cut off, and my normal hair grew out, I was in love. I would look lovingly at my hair in the mirror, for it was as beautiful to me as Connie Britton's.

I would play with it, braid it, and curl it. I wanted to shout from the rooftops, "MY HAIR IS AMAZING!" I am convinced there has never been anyone on Planet Earth who appreciated their hair as much as I do. It is stunning, even on its worst day.

I have learned to love my body, cherish it, and take care of it. Taking notice of sleep patterns, food dilemmas, and water intake. Knowing that how I care for myself matters, taking care of my body allows me to care for my family and my future. I try to eat and live as if I lived in one of the "blue zones," which refers to the now six places in the world with the longest-living and healthiest populations. I strive to eat a plant-based diet, with fresh fruit, veggies, nuts, legumes, and whole grains. I eat meat and fish on occasion, but not every day. I eat cake and cookies; I drink coffee and wine. Everything is in moderation and especially with friends.

I make sure to eat appropriate amounts of protein, especially on days I work out. I make going to the gym fun and a joy. I don't use working out as a punishment for eating, because it is not. I go to our local gym in the morning, when the average age of attendees is seventy. I walk on the track and notice the older ladies walking and talking together, the same people there every day. I tell them they are my inspiration; they encourage me to come back to the gym. Weight training for bone strength, stretching and balance work for mobility, and cardio to keep my heart working correctly.

All of it fits, and all of it contributes to helping me feel good in my body. I feel strong. I can ride my boys on my back if they get tired while we are hiking or at Dollywood, which is not something I could have done when I was fresh out of the hospital. The endorphins I gain from working out are the best payout, residual in my everyday life of running kids to and fro after school. Lucky for me, almost all of my best friends go to my gym, mixing health, wellness, and friendship into a brilliant adventure at every mutual workout.

Having these everyday friends is an essential component of my life, one of my greatest sources of appreciation. I can see how relationships with others played an integral role in my survival, and I never take it for granted. Human connection is vital for life.

The donated blood products that were used to keep me alive were gifts from strangers. Without donated blood, there is no hope for a leukemia patient, making blood and hope both fundamental for survival.

If leukemia rears its ugly head in my life again, the only thing that can save me is the marrow inside the bones of my younger brother, Erick. This is a beautiful example of how important human connection is, for our family, friends, and strangers alike. We need each other.

Sharing life with neighbors is not a new idea, but it is understated in importance. I have learned that community is our one chance to experience heaven on Earth. I live in a small, safe neighborhood, with retirees all around. I stand in my yard and talk with those who have walked many miles before me.

I glean their wisdom as we watch my boys play and ride bikes; their fine smile lines hold memories of their children playing on the same street. They gently guide me toward an appreciation for my stage of life, for they know the secret of young motherhood, how quickly it fades. They remind me I am never alone.

Throughout my exceptional life, I have learned that relationship with others is one of our greatest gifts. We were never meant to go at it alone. In my opinion, sitting on a porch with your people, laughing, and sharing a funny story, while your children play is the peak human experience.

I look in the mirror and I see chicken pox scars, fine smile lines, and freckles from the sun. I see sparse eyebrows, with roots weak from the attacks of chemotherapy. One of my eyelids is bigger than the other, same for my cheeks. My hair is turning gray, the white offshoots thick, wavy, and completely unruly. The half-a-trillion-dollar beauty industry welcomes me with open arms, a remedy for every occasion, and confirmation that it has discovered the "fountain of youth" and it only costs $19.99 plus shipping and handling. I notice the trend, the expectation of society for women in their thirties and forties to look twenty-six forever.

When I look in the mirror, I aspire to see the woman my mother sees and to love myself unconditionally. I imagine how much my abuelita and nannie love my face, as I love theirs. There is nothing I would change about their appearance—their faces depict their lifetimes of joy, struggle, and peace. Their wrinkles tell their stories. It is apparent to me that a wrinkle's best friend is wisdom, and you can't receive one without the other.

To live is to grow old. To survive all that life throws your way is to experience pain and joy, to gain sun spots and laugh lines. Wrinkles are an extrinsic expression of a life well lived and a soul well loved. The more I laugh, the deeper my smile lines grow, proof of my existence.

I could have easily been twenty-six forever, smooth skin pulled tautly. Stretched over my bones after fighting leukemia and being defeated by chemo; face on a funeral home pamphlet. Thanks be to God, I have the beautiful privilege of adding years and lines to my face. I must accept changes as they occur to my body and embrace the metamorphosis that time makes inevitable.

What do I desire out of this life? What is my hope?

More time, laughter, friends, family, and most of all, wrinkles.

If I look in the mirror and see wrinkles, that means I am alive.

For these reasons, I must shout from the rooftops, "Wrinkles welcome!

ACKNOWLEDGMENTS

*F*irst, I extend my deepest thanks to the Illumify Media team—Michael, Geoff, Karen, and Jen. Your support guided me every step of the way.

To my editor, Deb Hall: your seamless editing and encouragement bolstered my confidence as a writer. Thank you for caring for my words and story.

Brock Swinson, your invitation to join a non-fiction writing group provided the accountability I needed to complete the first draft. Thank you for that push.

Alex Billings, you boldly declared from the start of our friendship that I needed to write a book. This is all your fault. Thank you, lady.

Special thanks to the MVPs of my formative education: Ms. Whitten, Ms. Combs, Mr. Barrowclaugh, Ms. Moore, Ms. Thomas, Dr. Scott, Ms. Vaughn-Marion, Ms. Holland, Mr. Galloway, Ms. Soderberg, Ms. Carter, Coach Webster, and Jon and Misti Williams.

My professors at Gardner-Webb University significantly shaped my education. A heartfelt thanks to Dr. Blevins for introducing us to The Cure; Dr. Theado for assigning The Avett Brothers and affirming my writing; Dr. David Carscaddon, whose belief in me has been invaluable; and Dr. Laura Carscaddon, whose lessons in humanity and poise remain with me.

To my earliest readers and encouragers—Khouan, Hannah, Kathy, Meghan, Colin, Alma, Paul, Heidy, Karl, Sam, Katherine, Megan, Bree, Carrie, Martha, Ryan, Christi, Bailey, Josh, Rachel, and my Safe Space—your support has kept my heart full.

Lisa, thank you for allowing me to share the story of your beautiful daughter, Luci.

To the doctors, nurses, and staff at Atrium Health Wake Forest Baptist, you saved our family. A special thanks to Dr. Howard, Dr. Powell, NP Megan, and Dr. Hermes for your compassionate care.

My Hooker/Laurent/Alfaro family, I am blessed by each of you. Thank you for your love and safety throughout this journey.

Louis and Jack, you are my peace and joy. I love you both no matter what.

Joseph, my husband, and best friend, none of this would be possible without you. I am profoundly grateful for your unwavering support and love.

ABOUT THE AUTHOR

*G*aby Laurent lives in Oak Ridge, Tennessee, with her husband and two precious sons. A beacon of hope, Gaby is passionate about sharing her journey through life's challenges to inspire others. With a deep appreciation for the outdoors, you'll often find her tending to her garden and compost heap or walking while listening to a podcast.

Gaby holds a master's degree in school counseling, reflecting her commitment to supporting others on their journeys. Her greatest joys include sharing laughter with her husband and cherishing moments with friends and family as she embraces the beauty of life's simple pleasures.

You can find her on Instagram @gabylaurentwrites

*A*s I close this chapter of my life, I invite you to share your thoughts. Did these stories resonate with you? Did they inspire, challenge, or comfort you? Let me know by leaving a review with your preferred retailer or Goodreads.

Printed in the USA
CPSIA information can be obtained
at www.ICGtesting.com
LVHW040727041024
792624LV00008BA/794